7/16/97

Dear Ralph:

Obviously you don't have to read this book — you can teach it. Nevertheless, it is wit[h] pleasure that I give [you one] of our books.

Best Wishes,
Israel.

Dear Ralph:

7/16/97

You missed your calling. You should have been a professor. No doubt you know everything in this book — and probably can explain it better!

Best regards,
Allen

FINANCE AND ACCOUNTING
FOR
LAWYERS

Finance and Accounting
for
Lawyers

Allen Michel

Israel Shaked

Professors Allen Michel and Israel Shaked are
faculty members at Boston University's School of
Management and managing directors of The
Michel/Shaked Group.

Legal Financial Press
Boston, Massachusetts 02215

To Our Families

ISBN   0-9653140-0-6
Library of Congress Catalog Card No. 96-77089

Printed in the United States of America

1 2 3 4 5 DO 0 9 8 7 6

Preface

The language of finance and accounting is a basic tool in the world of law. Whether you are a corporate attorney or litigator, the elements of finance and accounting often play a key role.

As financial advisors to attorneys in dozens of matters nationwide, we've seen first hand the importance of understanding financial issues. Whether the matter is a straightforward damages case or a complex merger negotiation, the attorney's awareness of the financial implications of alternative courses of action is necessary to appropriately advise the client.

Based on years of working with attorneys, we have designed this book to cover a set of issues frequently encountered by the practicing attorney. The book is easy to read, practical and filled with examples. It covers numerous financial issues which are given scant attention in law schools in the United States. Specifically, Chapter 1 includes a discussion of the key financial statements produced by the firm. Importantly, it looks behind the numbers to enable the attorney to understand the true financial health and performance of a firm. It also provides a discussion of the Management Discussion and Analysis (MD&A) section of an annual report and the key financial issues necessary for the attorney involved in its preparation or review. Chapter 2 discusses time value of money and provides the attorney a way of evaluating the worth of funds received at different points in time. It is a key tool to the attorney involved in valuation issues, structured settlements or any matter where the value of future cash flows is a key ingredient. Securities are discussed in Chapter 3. In particular, the chapter provides an understanding of the relationship between risk and return, and provides an easy to use methodology to measure a security's performance. The chapter includes sections on stocks, fixed income securities, convertibles, warrants, options and other derivatives. Chapter 4 focuses on the cost of capital. It discusses the cost of equity capital, debt capital and the firm's overall cost of capital. Valuation issues are covered in Chapter 5. Numerous examples are provided and different approaches are explained. Chapter 6 details the calculation of damages in different scenarios. For example, it includes both contractual damages resulting from an operating business and also damages from securities losses. The final chapter, Chapter 7, describes financial issues associated with bankruptcy and fraudulent conveyance.

The task of putting together a comprehensive and readable finance and accounting book is a major undertaking. We owe a debt of gratitude to many people who have read the manuscript. In particular, we would like to thank Meir Amikam, Joseph Cortas, Donald Glockner, Richard Goldstein, Irwin Heller, Ryan Keating, Stephen Kempainen, Alberto Lage, Gene Landy, David Langlois, Judy Mencher, Olga Santoro, Terry Stewart, Pam Webster and Brian Whitely. We also thank Stephen Kempainen for his significant contribution to the chapter on financial statements.

We thank Darren Evans who patiently provided graphic guidance and word processing assistance on a never-ending set of drafts.

In particular, we would like to thank Dick Luecke for his cheerful guidance and never-ending source of wisdom. Most people find finance and accounting to be rather unexciting. However, Dick has a gift of bringing life to dull and colorless financial statements. He is a wordsmith extraordinaire.

We have used much of the material in the book both with our students and at financial seminars we have presented to our clients throughout the country. Through this process, we hope we have eliminated all errors. Naturally, it goes without saying that any misinterpretation or misstatement is greatly regretted.

Above all, we thank our families, who have tolerated countless discussions of virtually all the topics in this book.

FINANCE AND ACCOUNTING FOR LAWYERS

Table of Contents

Chapter One: The Basics of Financial Statements   1

Chapter Two: The Time Value of Money   63

Chapter Three: Securities   101

Chapter Four: The Cost of Capital   155

Chapter Five: Valuation   175

Chapter Six: Damages   211

Chapter Seven: Bankruptcy and Fraudulent Conveyances   239

Chapter 1
The Basics of Financial Statements

For those attorneys who managed to escape a course on financial accounting, or who have forgotten what they learned, this chapter is intended as a primer on financial statements and how they help us to interpret the economic status and performance of individual companies.

Financial statements are among the principal tools of finance. Investors use them to assess business performance and financial risk. Lenders use them to judge the creditworthiness of potential borrowers. Business executives use them to measure the progress of their firms, and often tie bonuses to specific information found in them. In legal matters involving mergers, acquisitions, valuations, bankruptcies, and damages, data contained in financial statements is essential.

This chapter is divided into two major parts. Part I examines the three primary financial statements: the balance sheet, the income statement, and the cash flow statement. It explains the purpose of each, and also discusses their limitations. And there are plenty of limitations.

In Part II, we will show you how data in these statements and other information can be used to assess business performance. For the practicing attorney, familiarity with the tools used to assess business performance is highly useful in a great number of situations involving acquisitions, divestitures, buy-sell arrangements, MD&As, bankruptcies, cases of fraudulent conveyance, and numerous others.

Before describing financial statements or their use, let's consider some basic methodologies and concepts used by accountants.

ACCRUAL VERSUS CASH METHOD

Many individuals and some small businesses keep track only of cash receipts and cash payments. This type of accounting is called *cash accounting.* Under the cash method, a company records sales when the cash is received and expenses when they are paid. Liabilities are recorded only when an obligation of a contractual nature is created (e.g. borrowing money from a bank).

The *accrual method* of accounting is different. It recognizes revenues and expenses as they are earned or incurred, even though they may not have been received or paid in cash. For example, a company using the accrual method will record the revenue from a sale when it invoices and ships a truckload of products to a customer, even though the cash payment will not be made for another 30 days. While most individuals and personal service providers adopt the cash method in reporting their personal income taxes, corporations generally use the accrual method. Because of its complexity, some practitioners refer to it as "a cruel method."

THE NINE BASIC ACCOUNTING CONCEPTS

There are nine concepts about financial statements that accountants view as the backbone of their profession:

1. *Dual-aspect concept.* This concept supports an equation that is fundamental and governs all accounting: assets = liabilities + equity. The fact that total assets must equal, or balance, total liabilities plus equity is why the balance sheet was given its name. The concept sounds simple, but it has provided

countless headaches for accountants and attorneys alike.

2. *Money-measurement concept.* Accounting reports present only line-items that can be expressed in dollars, such as sales or net income. One can thus add or subtract one item from another. If items, such as customer satisfaction, cannot be expressed in monetary terms, they cannot be reported. Thus, accounting is an incomplete record of the status of a business and, despite what many believe, does not always reveal important facts about a business.

3. *Entity concept.* Accounts are kept for entities (businesses), rather than for the persons who own, operate, or otherwise are associated with them. A business may be organized under any one of several legal forms, including a corporation, a partnership, or a sole proprietorship. Most often tax and liability issues dictate the choice.

4. *Going-concern concept.* Accounting assumes that an organization will continue to operate indefinitely unless there is evidence to the contrary. If the organization is on its last leg and not a going-concern, special accounting rules apply. Moreover, because of the going-concern concept, accounting does not report what the assets could be sold for if the organization ceased to exist, (e.g. if it was liquidated or merged with another entity).

5. *Cost concept.* Accounting focuses on the cost of assets, rather than on their market value. When a company buys an asset, it records the amount of the

asset at its cost. The amount for which an asset could be sold in the marketplace is called its market value. Some assets wear out and inflation affects the value of some assets. For these and other reasons, the market value of assets changes as time passes. However, accounting does not attempt to trace changes in the market value of most assets. Instead, accounting focuses on the historical cost of assets. For example, a piece of land bought for a few thousand dollars 50 years ago is thus valued on the company's books at the price then paid, rather than the $15 million it is valued at today, reflecting the location of the land at the intersection of two major interstate highways.

6. *Conservatism concept.* Accountants recognize increases in equity only when they are reasonably certain. They recognize decreases in equity as soon as they have occurred. For example, suppose that in January a manufacturer has good reason to believe that one of its customers will fail to pay a $100,000 bill, but that it will only be certain of this failure to pay in March. Conservatism requires that the decrease in equity (i.e. a bad debt expense) be recognized in January.

7. *Materiality concept.* Accountants may disregard immaterial transactions. Financial statements must disclose all material facts – i.e., those transactions that make a difference in understanding an entity's financial affairs. For example, if a large fraction of a firm's inventory is found to be worthless, the materiality concept requires that this fact be recorded. However, deciding which transactions are material

is a matter of judgment and often results in seemingly endless litigation.

8. *Realization concept.* This concept is concerned with the timing of revenues or costs. Consider revenues, for example. Revenue is recognized in the period in which it is realized. Both goods and services are products and the general rule is to recognize revenue from a product sale when the product is delivered. Revenue may be recognized before, during, or after the cash from the sale is received. Revenue is recognized before cash is received when a sale is made on credit. Revenue is recognized at the same time cash is received when the company delivers its product and the customer pays for it immediately. Revenue is recognized after the cash is received when the company receives the cash before delivering the product to the customer. Except for down payments, most companies' chief financial officers only dream about the day this will happen.

9. *Matching concept.* Under the accrual method, accountants match up costs and the revenues they produce. Costs associated with the revenues of a period are matched with the expenses of that period. For example, assume that a computer retailer bought computer hardware for $60,000 in July and sold it (i.e. delivered to a customer) for $75,000 in August. At the end of July the hardware was still in inventory, so its cost was not yet expensed. In August, the retailer records revenue of $75,000 and cost of goods sold (an expense) of $60,000. The $60,000 of expense relates to the sale of $75,000 and is matched against the revenue.

PART I: FINANCIAL STATEMENTS

Accounting information is provided by reports called financial statements. Generally Accepted Accounting Principles (GAAP) require companies to prepare three different statements. They are the balance sheet, the income statement, and the cash flow statement. Collectively, these tell the informed reader what a company owns and what it owes as of a particular date, its level of revenues, expenses and profits for a particular period, and the sources and uses of cash used over that same period.

As you will see, even within the GAAP rules that govern how financial statements are created, there is some "wiggle room" – enough room that Abraham Briloff warned that "financial statements are like fine perfume: to be sniffed but not swallowed."

THE BALANCE SHEET

The balance sheet is the first of the Big Three financial statements we will consider. In a nutshell, it is a "snapshot" revealing what assets a company owned and how those assets were financed at a given point in time, either with the funds of the owners or with other people's money. Looked at another way, it indicates a company's assets and the claims against them. The fact that total assets must equal total liabilities plus equity is why the statement is called a balance sheet. Consider the balance sheet for Harbor Systems Corporation, a firm that provides architectural engineering computer systems and software, over a period of three years. Although the investor is often concerned with performance only in the most recent period (Year 3), the listing of several years' balance sheets on one statement is useful in company analysis.

The purpose of the balance sheet is to present a firm's financial position as of a particular date (normally year-end) in terms of economic resources (assets), economic obligations (liabilities) and the residual claims of owners (the owners' equity).   Thus, the balance sheet takes the form of a simple equation:

$$\text{Assets} = \text{Liabilities} + \text{Owners' Equity}$$

It is amazing that such a simple equation is the backbone of our economic system.

Assets and liabilities are usually shown in the order of their liquidity – that is, the ease with which they can be turned into cash – with the most liquid assets (current assets) and liabilities (current liabilities) being shown first. By definition, owners' equity equals total assets less total liabilities.

Most items on a balance sheet are summaries of more detailed accounts. For example, cash is probably located in several separate bank accounts, but only the total of all these accounts is presented on the balance sheet.

Assets: Most firms need cash, inventory and other resources in order to operate. These resources are the firm's assets which it owns. Its employees, although perhaps its most valuable resource, are not accounting assets. It may seem strange that an accountant may not consider such a valuable resource as an asset on the balance sheet. To count as an asset, an item must pass two tests:

Exhibit 1-1. Harbor Systems Corporation Balance Sheets*

	Year 1	Year 2	Year 3
Current Assets:			
Cash	$ 63,713	$ 100,480	$ 402,448
Accounts Receivable	789,041	1,218,082	2,016,986
Inventory	138,977	237,772	462,118
Prepaid Expenses	75,000	100,000	215,000
Total Current Assets	1,066,732	1,656,334	3,096,552
Fixed Assets:			
Leasehold Improvements	57,997	122,622	298,269
Other Assets:			
Software	117,003	247,378	601,731
Total Assets	**$ 1,241,732**	**$ 2,026,334**	**$ 3,996,552**
Current Liabilities:			
Accounts Payable	196,554	297,491	504,517
Notes Payable-Bank	0	459,000	1,520,000
Notes Payable-Stockholders	77,000	229,350	757,200
Total Current Liabilities	273,554	985,841	2,781,717
Stockholders' Equity:			
Paid-In Capital	850,000	850,000	850,000
Retained Earnings	118,178	190,493	364,835
Total Stockholders' Equity	968,178	1,040,493	1,214,835
Total Liabilities and Equity	**$ 1,241,732**	**$ 2,026,334**	**$ 3,996,552**

* Numbers may not sum due to rounding.

1. An item must be controlled by the company. Usually this means that the company must own the item. Naturally there are exceptions to every rule, and certain long-term leases, referred to by the accounting brigade as capital leases, fit the bill to be considered an exception.
2. The item must be valuable to the entity. This requires that the item must have been acquired at a measurable cost. You are probably asking now what an immeasurable cost is. For example, if a software vendor bought the rights to sell software from another company for $200,000, the rights would be an asset. However, if the same vendor had built up an excellent reputation for high quality products and service, this reputation would not count as an asset.

As you will notice in Exhibit 1-1, assets are classified as either being current or noncurrent. Current assets are those assets that are expected to be converted into cash or sold or consumed within the near future, usually within one year. Normally, these include cash, marketable securities, accounts receivable, inventory and prepaid expenses. Let us consider the details of each.

- *Cash* is money on hand and money in bank accounts that can be withdrawn at any time. When an organization writes a check, the amount of its cash is not actually reduced on the bank's records until the check has been cashed. Nevertheless, the usual practice is to record a decrease in cash on the day the check is issued. Thus, while the cash balance has remained unchanged, the firm's book balance has been reduced by the amount of the check. This is often relevant in situations where a lawyer is tracing the flow of funds.

- *Marketable securities* are securities that are expected to be converted into cash within one year, (e.g. treasury bills, certificates of deposit). An organization owns these securities so as to earn a return on funds that otherwise would be doing the corporate equivalent of being stowed under the mattress.
- An *account receivable* is an amount owed to the company, usually by one of its customers as a result of purchasing goods and/or services. Accounts receivable are recorded as a current asset when a firm sells (records revenue) a product to a customer and the customer does not pay the bill immediately (i.e. sold on credit). Dramatic increases in this asset without corresponding increases in sales may signal a red flag for the firm. On one hand, it is not receiving funds from its customers, but on the other hand, its suppliers expect to get paid. A liquidity crisis may be around the corner.

  Since accounts receivable include amounts from customers who probably will never pay their bills, some estimate for uncollectible accounts (i.e. bad debts) should be recorded. Accountants usually do not decrease the accounts receivable account directly since they do not know exactly which customers will not pay their bills. Therefore, a separate account called Allowance for Doubtful Accounts is used to record the decrease in accounts receivable (and thus, a decrease in revenue).
- *Inventory* represents finished goods being held for sale, work-in-progress as well as partially finished products, raw materials, and supplies. Inventory increases when the quantity of these items held by the firm increases and decreases when they are sold to

customers, thus becoming "cost of goods sold." Like sizable increases in accounts receivable, large increases in inventory without increases in sales often provide useful information about the company's impending liquidity to an attorney assessing the firm's cash position.

- *Prepaid expenses* is the name given to intangible assets that will be consumed in the near future. A company often purchases insurance protection prior to the period covered by the policy. This policy is an asset, though an intangible one. If it covers a short period of time, it is a current asset. Besides insurance policies, prepaid expenses may consist of rent and advertising expenses which have been paid in advance. Prepaid expenses increase when such an item is purchased in advance and decrease when a portion of it is used (as time passes).

- *Noncurrent assets*, as the name suggests, are those that are expected to be useful for longer than one year. Noncurrent assets normally refer to property, plant and equipment, long-term investments, patents and trademarks, and goodwill. For a company like Harbor, noncurrent assets would typically consist of owned property and buildings, leasehold improvements if the office space is leased, and software development costs. Leasehold improvements may be modifications/enhancements to leased premises. Owned buildings, equipment and leasehold improvements are depreciated (reduced) over the useful life of the asset or lease (i.e. depreciation expense is recorded on the income statement over the useful life of the asset). Goodwill arises when one company buys another company and pays more than the book value of its assets. It is amortized (similar to depreciation) over a period not to exceed 40 years. While accountants have a set of rules and guidelines to measure the book value of non-current assets, the true market value of those assets is often difficult to determine. It is particularly difficult to precisely assess the value of an intangible asset such as goodwill. It is not unusual to see situations where the price paid for a company differs markedly from the firm's value based upon the numbers on the company's books. Indeed, in a discussion of a series of lawsuits about the issue of goodwill arising from acquisitions, The Wall Street Journal asks, ". . . how could accounting air turn into billions?"

STRAIGHT-LINE AND ACCELERATED DEPRECIATION

Companies depreciate assets like buildings, vehicles, and equipment on either a "straight-line" or an "accelerated" basis. The straight-line basis is simple to understand. If a piece of equipment is expected to have a five year productive life, its book value is reduced by one-fifth each year. Thus, if a piece of equipment is put on the books at its original cost of, say, $100,000, the company would depreciate it by $20,000 in each of five years. The $20,000 would be used to reduce the company's taxable income in each year.

Because of the time value of money, people would rather reduce taxes in the near term, even if they must pay the same total taxes over the life of the asset. Thus, the appeal of accelerated depreciation is the possibility to write off larger amounts in the early years. For example, one accelerated depreciation method is called the "double declining balance" method. It uses twice the straight-line rate. In our example above, double declining balance would write off two-fifths of the original cost the first year, or $40,000, leaving the equipment with a book value of just $60,000. During the second year, it writes off two-fifths of this, or $24,000. And so on. By the third year, the write-offs from this accelerated method are less than the straight-line method: $14,400. They will continue to drop, with the remaining book value deducted fully in the fifth year, making the asset fully depreciated.

Liabilities. Liabilities describe what a company owes to suppliers, employees, the tax authorities, lenders, and others. For Harbor Systems, liabilities are clear and straightforward. It has three "current" liabilities – again, items due within a year – and no long-term obligations. Companies with more complex balance sheets may list liabilities for bonds, pensions, reserves against future warranty claims, and deferred employee compensation, among others. While most firms have some long-term obligations, not all do. Indeed, some choose to limit their long-term debt because of the conservative nature of the firm's senior management. Others keep their long-term debt limited due to the inherent operating risk of the business. High-technology firms, for example, are often reluctant to add significant financial risk associated with long-term debt to the already high operating risk of the organization.

Current liabilities are obligations of the firm which become due within a short time period, usually within one year. For Harbor Systems, current liabilities are:

- *Accounts Payable.* These are the opposite of accounts receivable; that is, they are amounts that the company owes its suppliers for having received goods or services. The stretching of accounts payable is often one of the first signs of financial weakness in an organization. Attorneys beware. It is a warning that cash flows may be slowing.
- *Notes Payable-Bank* and *Notes Payable-Stockholders.* They are reported separately from accounts payable because the debt is evidenced by a promissory note and is often collateralized by the company's assets.
- Other items may be classified as current liabilities. They include amounts owed to employees and others for services they have performed, taxes owed the government, and advances collected from customers before delivery of the product. These items are commonly referred to as *accrued liabilities.*

Current liabilities may also include portions of long-term debt which are expected to be paid within the next year. The level of current liabilities fluctuates with the level of business and short-term borrowing activity.

Although Harbor Systems reports no long-term debt, noncurrent liabilities typically include the portion of any funds borrowed by the company which are not due within the next year, including bonds, mortgages, and long-term bank borrowing. Debt increases when additional funds are borrowed and decreases when the company makes payments on the debt.

Owners' (or Stockholders') Equity. The other source of funds that an entity uses to finance its assets is called *equity*. Equity consists of capital obtained from sources other than creditors and other liabilities. Here are the ones listed on Harbor Systems' balance sheet:

- Equity investors provide funds for which they receive common stock. The total amount of funds supplied by equity investors is called *Paid-In Capital*. While this amount reflects the amount paid into the firm by its equity investors, it may bear scant resemblance to today's market value of the company.
- Equity funds also come from a second source, the profits or earnings generated by the company. The amount of earnings that has not been distributed to equity investors is retained in the company and is called *Retained Earnings*. Retained earnings are additions to capital that have been accumulated since the firm began operations and are not necessarily earnings of a single year.

Retained earnings is a regular source of confusion and error for the unwary, who often view it as the corporate "piggy bank." In fact, any of our finance students who suggests that new equipment can be financed with funds drawn out of retained earnings is put on bread and water for a week! Interestingly, it is not unusual to find firms whose retained earnings have been sizable at the time of their bankruptcy filing. It must be remembered that retained earnings is not cash.

For balance sheet purposes, the amount reported as retained earnings (RE) for a given year is the sum of retained earnings for the previous year plus earnings after taxes (EAT) for this year, less any cash dividends paid during this year.

$$\boxed{\text{RE this year} = \text{RE last year} + \text{EAT this year} - \text{Dividends this year}}$$

If we rearrange the terms of our basic balance sheet equation just a bit, to

$$\boxed{\text{Assets - Liabilities = Owners' Equity}}$$

we can see that owners' equity is a residual – what remains for the shareholders after all claims of non-owners against the company's assets are satisfied. And since creditors can sue a company when amounts due to them are not paid, equity investors do in fact stand at the end of the line in terms of claims against a company's assets.

THE ACCOUNTING VALUE VS. THE ECONOMIC VALUE OF BALANCE SHEET ITEMS

What you see as values on the balance sheet may not represent true economic value. There is often a substantial difference between the accounting value of a company's assets and their true economic, or market, value. The practice of representing balance sheet items at original, or historical, cost is a key source of this disparity. Harbor Systems, for example, may have over $400,000 of software and computer equipment in its warehouse, but the market value of these items may be significantly less due to product obsolescence in its high-paced field. Another company may have land and buildings on its books as fixed assets, but the market value of these properties may also be quite different from how they are represented on the balance sheet. Accounting conventions depreciate the value of real property according to an IRS approved accounting and tax schedule. Yet in reality, the value of the company's land and buildings may be rising at double-digit rates.

So why does the accounting profession use historical cost? The answer is that market values for many balance sheet items are difficult to obtain and verify, and susceptible to manipulation. Accountants would rather be consistently wrong following a uniform method than allow suspicious values to find their way into the balance sheet.

A few balance sheet items, however, are "marked to the market." For example, if a company holds marketable financial instruments (stocks, treasuries, bonds) among its assets, their market value can be verified.

Many companies have intangible assets: patents, brand names, proprietary technologies, and the business know-how of its employees. "Goodwill," is one of the intangible assets often seen in financial statements. It is understood to be a function of the economic value of a company, its brand name or customer loyalty. This value is presented on the balance sheet when the asset has been acquired for more than its book value. For example, if Harbor Systems had acquired a small distributor for $1 million when the distributor's book value was only $800 thousand, the excess ($200 thousand) would be represented on Harbor's balance sheet as "goodwill." And like other assets, it would be "amortized" on a regular basis. (For intangible assets, accountants use the term amortization instead of depreciation). And again, these balance sheet values may or may not have much to do with true economic value. The value of goodwill and other intangible assets is rarely recognized except in cases of takeovers and mergers.

With all of these deficiencies, one wonders about the usefulness of balance sheet representation of company assets. The truth is that in cases involving damages and

WHAT IS A BRAND NAME WORTH?

Brand names are viewed as important assets by corporate managers, who go to great lengths to protect and enhance their values. Nevertheless, these assets are rarely reflected on the balance sheet. As outsiders, we seldom appreciate their magnitudes until a merger or acquisition is made and the financial terms of the deal are made public.

One of the most spectacular deals was Philip Morris's purchase of Kraft, the cheese and food products maker. In addition to its many Kraft brands, the company also owned Miracle Whip and Breyer's ice cream. Philip Morris paid $1.3 billion for Kraft – four times the balance sheet value of Kraft's assets.

valuations, quite often the value of many assets must be adjusted to reflect true economic value. Subsequent chapters will show how these adjustments are made.

THE INCOME STATEMENT

While the balance sheet is a point-in-time picture of what a company owns and what it owes, the income statement describes the results of operations for a given period, normally one year. Some people call it a profit & loss statement, or "P&L." By whatever name, its purpose is to measure the earnings (or profits) of the company during a particular time period.

The income statement presents the significant components of net income, usually in order of their magnitude. For most companies, these are revenues from sales, the cost of goods sold, and a number of operating expenses. Other income statement items typically include general and administrative expenses, interest expenses, taxes, and realized gains and losses from the disposal of assets. Net income – the proverbial "bottom line" – is a residual, what is left of a company's revenues and other income after all of its cost of goods sold, expenses, costs of doing business, and taxes are taken out. Net income may be either reinvested in operations, put in the bank, or paid out to shareholders.

We can present this flow of resources as follows:

	Sales revenues
-	Cost of goods sold
-	Operating expenses
+	Non-operating income
-	Taxes
=	Net income (profits or earnings)

Now consider the income statements for Harbor Systems Corporation in Exhibit 1-2. Note that the statements present activities for a particular time frame. The two previous years are also presented to make comparison and analysis easier. They report sales, but are broken out by product. Cost of goods sold, as well, provides a breakout by product line. Operating expenses are of several types, including overhead costs of occupancy and salaries.

After reducing revenues by all of the firm's costs and expenses, including interest and taxes, we finally reach the bottom line, representing net income for the period. Because accountants and financial types are more interested in numbers than words, some of their terms lack precision.

Exhibit 1-2. Harbor Systems Corporation 3-Year Income Statements.

Sales:	Year 1	Year 2	Year 3
Software Sales	$ 1,680,000	$ 2,297,100	$ 3,190,200
Hardware Sales	600,000	1,037,400	2,024,550
Aftermarket Sales	120,000	370,500	920,250
Total Sales	2,400,000	3,705,000	6,135,000
Cost of Goods Sold:			
Software Sales	683,256	901,842	1,269,061
Hardware Sales	486,420	832,202	1,617,413
Aftermarket Sales	26,028	75,693	182,670
Total Cost of Goods Sold	1,195,704	1,809,737	3,069,144
Gross Profit	1,204,296	1,895,263	3,065,856
Operating Expenses:*			
Salaries and Benefits	725,410	1,174,729	1,975,708
Advertising and Promotion	48,000	74,100	184,050
Travel	24,000	37,050	61,350
Occupancy	103,630	108,812	114,252
Software Development	135,260	171,614	134,275
Total Operating Expenses	1,036,300	1,566,305	2,469,635
Earnings Before Interest and Taxes	167,996	328,958	596,221
Interest Expense	7,700	68,835	227,720
Earnings Before Taxes	160,296	260,123	368,501
Income Taxes	64,118	104,049	147,401
Net Income	**$ 96,178**	**$ 156,074**	**$ 221,100**

* For the sake of simplicity, depreciation and amortization were excluded from the income statement.

Thus, the terms *profit, earnings* and *income* are often used interchangeably to represent the difference between revenues and expenses. Obviously, if attorneys had invented this system, more attention would have been paid to the language. Most income statement terminology, however, has a clear meaning, and we present several key terms below.

Revenues. Recall that the realization concept governs the recognition of revenue. Revenue from products sold or services rendered should be recognized in the income statement as earned in the period the product was sold and delivered or the service was rendered. For example, a firm might record revenues from software and hardware when it installed a system for a customer. It is easy to fall into a trap believing that revenue is cash. Remember, however, that most companies sell on credit, with revenue merely representing the sale, not the receipt of payment.

Costs and expenses. The matching concept governs the recognition of expenses. Just as revenues in a period are not necessarily the same as cash receipts for the same period, the expenses of a period are not the same as the cash payments in that period. When a company purchases goods and services, it makes an expenditure. Once the items for which the expenditures are made are consumed, the expenditures become expenses. For example, assume that Harbor Systems made an expenditure of $50,000 for the purchase of inventory in July and $30,000 of those goods were actually sold in July. As a result, $30,000 becomes an expense in July. The remaining $20,000 of goods still remained in inventory as an asset. Therefore, the expenditures of a period are either expenses of the period or assets at the end of the period. When an asset is consumed in the operations of a business, an expense is incurred. Thus, an expenditure occurs when the asset is acquired and an expense is generated when the asset is consumed, both of which may take place in the same period.

THE EXPENSING OF THE BALANCE SHEET ITEMS

Buildings, equipment and inventory are tangible balance sheet assets. Depreciation expense describes the cost of consuming buildings and equipment. For example, a machine that costs $5,000 and is expected to last five years would have depreciation expense of $1,000 recorded each year for five years under the straight-line method. The protection provided by an insurance policy is an intangible asset, yet its expense is recorded as prepaid insurance expense. While Harbor Systems has no significant depreciable assets, firms that do, not only reduce the value of these assets on the balance sheet over time, but also reflect those wasting values as expenses on the income statement as "depreciation expense," "insurance expense," and so forth. Notice that unlike salaries and travel, there is no out-of-pocket cash outflow associated with either of these two expenses.

Liabilities for expenses incurred but not yet paid for are called *accrued liabilities*, or simply accruals. An example of an accrued liability which results in an expense is the cost of salaries and benefits earned by employees which have not been paid by the company. In this instance, the company records an expense and an accrued liability for the amount earned by the employees. The accrued liability would be removed once the salaries and benefits had been paid. Large increases in accruals should raise questions about when they must be paid down and how the firm will obtain the funds to meet its obligations at the time the accruals must be paid.

ECONOMIC VS. ACCOUNTING EARNINGS

Just as the conventions of accounting have given us balance sheets that fail to truly reflect economic realities, the eye-shade brigade has likewise produced income statements that are not quite what they seem. Similar deviations from economic reality are often observed in the use of historical cost and methods used to depreciate or amortize the value of assets.

Income and historical cost. While usually the true value of a dollar of revenue that hits the cash register during an accounting period is a dollar, the cost matched against this dollar is subject to some accounting manipulation.

Example. Due to a vendor's bankruptcy, Harbor Systems was able to purchase several hundred units of networking software for a fire sale price of only $50 per unit. As the new year began, the warehouse had a large inventory of these units. Subsequent purchases of that same software from other vendors had to be made at the normal but higher price of $80 per unit. The result was that Harbor's warehouse contained units of the same item at very different costs, even though the units were otherwise identical.

"So what?" you're probably asking. As these software units are sold and shipped over the course of the year, which cost should Harbor match against its revenues, $50 or $80? Or does it matter – it's all networking software?

In fact, it does matter for the bottom line. If the company matches its $50 units against revenues – a matching approach called "first in, first out" (FIFO) – then the company will have greater profits to report and higher taxes to pay. If it chooses to match its $80 software against revenues – a matching process called "last in, first out" (LIFO) – then bottom line earnings and taxes will be reduced. The difference between these two approaches is illustrated by Exhibit 1-3.

Exhibit 1-3. LIFO vs. FIFO

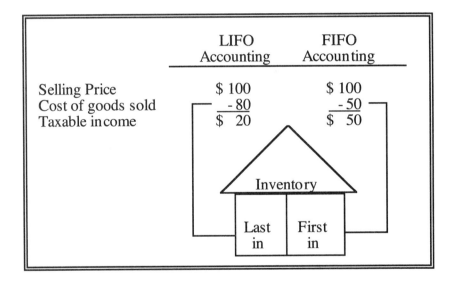

Notice that the economics of these transactions are the same. All that differs is the accounting income. Accounting conventions and IRS rules allow companies some discretion over using FIFO or LIFO methods as long as they remain fairly consistent. It is the company that uses FISH that often finds itself in trouble – First In Still Here!

GAMES PEOPLE PLAY

If you are like most people, you already understand the practical art of juggling payments and receipts to minimize federal income taxes. If you need more tax deductions in a given year, you will write those charitable checks before the end of the tax year slips by. And around mid-December you'll tell your clients "Hey, it's the holiday season. Don't pay me until January," which spares you a tax liability for this year.

Businesses play the same game, but not simply to defer taxes. Managers have performance and bonus goals tied to accounting revenues and/or earnings. Mid-way into the fourth quarter, managers watch "the numbers" with growing desperation. They start hammering on sales reps to push merchandise out to customers, even if special incentives or discounts are required. Consumer goods manufacturers "load" distribution channels with merchandise in order to boost their year-end numbers. They will do whatever it takes to book revenues or boost earnings – sometimes even when they know that merchandise will come back as "returns" after year-end. But that is another accounting year with lots of time left to play the game.

In addition to the gamesmanship of income reporting, Generally Accepted Accounting Principles are sufficiently flexible that companies have a degree of discretion with respect to determining earnings. Depending on how they choose to handle revenue recognition, depreciation, FIFO or LIFO treatment of inventories, and so forth, companies can – to some degree – reduce earnings (to reduce tax liabilities) or boost earnings (to make management performance look good to shareholders).

How net income finds its way back to the balance sheet. The net income of a company at year-end must be reflected somewhere on the balance sheet. Well, not all of it. If a company distributes some of its earnings to stockholders in the form of cash dividends, those funds disappear. But what remains, as we learned earlier, is added to the previous year's (which is the same as saying the beginning of this year's) retained earnings to produce the current year's retained earnings.

Our friends at Harbor Systems produced net income of $221,100 in Year 3. What you do not see in these statements is the fact that they distributed $46,758 of that income to stockholders. How do you know? Retained earnings at the end of year 2 were $190,493. Year 3's net income was $221,100. Thus, if Harbor Systems would not have paid any dividends, its end of year 3 retained earnings would have been $411,593 ($190,493 + $221,100). However, end of year 3's balance sheet indicates retained earnings of only $364,835, which is $46,758 short of the $411,593 figure. Hence, $46,758 in dividends were paid.

THE CASH FLOW STATEMENT

With all the qualifications attached to numbers in the balance sheet and income statement, attorneys who read financial statements have found it useful to know where the cash comes from and where it goes during a given accounting period. The accounting profession has obliged with the cash flow statement. Simply put, the cash flow statement indicates the sources and uses of cash for a period of time (normally one year). The net cash flow for the period is then added to (or subtracted from) the beginning of the period cash balance in order to arrive at the ending cash balance.

Exhibit 1-4. Harbor Systems Corporation: 3-year Cash Flow Statement

	Year 1	Year 2	Year 3
Net Income	$ 96,178	$ 156,074	$ 221,100
Changes in Working Capital:			
Decrease (Increase) in:			
Accounts Receivable	-512,877	-429,041	-798,904
Inventory	-38,977	-98,795	-224,346
Prepaid Expenses	-15,000	-25,000	-115,000
Increase (Decrease) in:			
Accounts Payable	141,321	100,937	207,026
Cash Flow From Operations	-329,355	-295,825	-710,124
Investing Activities:			
Leasehold Improvements	7,003	-64,625	-175,647
Purchase of Software	-37,003	-130,375	-354,353
Cash Flow From Investing Activities	-30,000	-195,000	-530,000
Financing Activities:			
Proceeds from Notes Payable-Bank	0	459,000	1,061,000
Proceeds from Notes Payable-Stockholders	77,000	152,350	527,850
Distribution to Stockholders	0	-83,758	-46,758
Cash Flow From Financing Activities	77,000	527,592	1,542,092
Net Cash Flow	-282,355	36,767	301,968
Cash At Beginning Of Year	346,068	63,713	100,480
Cash At End Of Year	$ 63,713	$ 100,480	$ 402,448

As presented in Exhibit 1-4, the statement of cash flow is broken down into three sections which allows the reader to determine how and where the particular company obtained funds and where it used funds.

From operations. The first section shows cash flow from operations. This is determined by adjusting net income (net loss) for the period for noncash expenses (e.g. depreciation, amortization) and changes in working capital. Working capital is defined as current assets less current liabilities. If current assets, excluding cash, increase, then there is a use of cash.

> **Example.** If accounts receivable increase, to obtain the cash flow, the increase in receivables should be subtracted from net income, accounting for the fact that some of the revenues which have been recorded in the income statement have not yet been collected. If accounts receivable are decreasing, payments from customers are coming in at a faster rate than credit sales are recorded on the firm's books. In other words, to determine the firm's cash flow, the firm must add the decrease in accounts receivable to its net income. Thus, when current assets such as accounts receivable or inventory increase, cash is used to finance the receivables or purchase inventory, and thus cash flow is reduced. When current assets decrease, cash flow correspondingly increases. Similarly, if current liabilities increase, the increase is treated as a source of cash. An increase in accounts payable means that vendors are funding the purchase of goods and services and as a result supply cash to the firm. Therefore, the increase in accounts payable must be added to the net income in order to arrive at the firm's cash flow. The opposite adjustment is made when current liabilities decrease. The bottom line of the working capital discussion is that increases in working capital must be funded by

cash. Sizable increases in working capital needs can result in a cash squeeze, leaving the firm either temporarily or permanently impaired.

For Harbor, in year 3, both net income and accounts payable contributed positively to cash flows from operations. But an overwhelming increase in current assets resulted in a negative total cash flow from operations, ($710,124).

From investing. The next section of the cash flow statement focuses on the company's investing activities. Investing activities normally include investments in, or disposals of, fixed assets. Harbor has sold no assets but has made sizable investments in its leasehold improvements and software purchases. Thus, it has negative cash flow from investing equal to $530 thousand.

From financing. The final section of the cash flow statement highlights the company's financing activities. Financing activities include payments made on borrowings, additional borrowings taken out during the period, the issuance of additional equity (stock) and distributions to owners (e.g. cash dividends). Harbor has taken in cash as a result of borrowing from its bank and its stockholders. These positive cash flows were reduced by $46,758 distributed to stockholders, leaving the company's total cash flow from financing at over $1.5 million.

In sum, the cash flow statement adds the cash flows of these three sets of activities to produce *net cash flow*. This figure, $301,968 for Harbor, is then added to the cash balance at the beginning of the year to produce the year-end cash position of approximately $402,448. (Notice how this same number appears under current assets on the balance sheet.)

OTHER FINANCIAL DOCUMENTS

In addition to the financial statements just discussed, the Securities and Exchange Commission (SEC) requires publicly-owned companies to file a number of documents containing financial information, including:

Form 8-K. An 8-K must be filed whenever a publicly-owned company experiences an event that could materially affect its financial situation or the value of its shares. These events may include merger or divestiture or some change in the corporate bylaws. Form 8-K must be filed within one month of the event and must be followed by a public announcement.

Form 10-K. Every exchange-listed company with 500 or more shareholders or $1 million or more assets is required to file an annual Form 10-K with the SEC. This document contains the material required in annual reports to shareholders as well as some additional specific information such as five-year sales by product classes and by separate lines of business.

Form 10-Q. Companies required to file a 10-K are also required to file a 10-Q, a quarterly report which need not be audited.

Prospectus on New Securities. As part of its authority to require "full disclosure" of material information from companies seeking to sell securities to the public, the SEC requires that every new issue be described in a prospectus, known as a "red herring." A prospectus is a formal description of the offer, the history and operations of the offering company, the company's plans, the background of its management, and other material information that investors should be provided with prior to making reasoned investment decisions.

All of these documents are publicly available.

MANAGEMENT'S DISCUSSION AND ANALYSIS OF THE FIRM'S FINANCIAL CONDITION AND THE RESULTS OF OPERATIONS: MD&A

The MD&A section of the annual report gives management an opportunity to describe the firm's financial statements in narrative form. The SEC requires such a meaningful discussion because the numerical presentation and associated footnotes may be insufficient to provide the investor with a satisfactory understanding of the firm's financial and operating condition. The content of the MD&A has evolved since 1980 when the SEC revised Regulation S-K and adopted Item 303. During the 1980's, all the SEC actions relating to MD&A deficiencies were brought together with other security law violations, typically fraud.

The first case brought by the SEC solely on the issue of MD&A related to Caterpillar Tractor's lack of disclosure of the stability of earnings generated by its Brazilian subsidiary. Since then, the SEC has brought an increasing number of cases, including:

Salant Corporation – The SEC accused Salant of failing to discuss "known uncertainties" relating to its declining financial situation. The agency indicated that the firm knew of its declining liquidity because:

a)   it had relaxed its financial covenants in credit agreements which it revised;

b)   it suffered significant declines in operating results;

c)   it delayed payments to its suppliers;

d)   it had short-term funding needs.

America West – The company suffered financial losses and was unable to comply with its debt covenants and ultimately filed Chapter XI. However, in its 10Q, it made little mention of the impending crisis and the likelihood of complying with the covenants and obtaining financing.

Del-Val Financial Corporation – The SEC found that the firm's treasurer knew that the firm was in the midst of serious liquidity problems. Yet it only disclosed that liquidity might suffer if certain unlikely contingencies would occur.

Each of these situations suggests that the SEC is concerned that insufficient information about known conditions or trends is presented in the MD&A. Indeed, regulations S-K and subsequent interpretive releases define specific types of disclosures which must be made.

In particular, the MD&A requires a discussion of material changes in liquidity, capital resources and results of operations. Item 303 of Regulation S-K requires disclosure of forward-looking information including any "known trends or any known demands, commitments, events or uncertainties that will result in or that are reasonably likely to result in the registrant's liquidity increasing or decreasing in any material way. Similar disclosures relating to

capital resources and continuing operations are also required. An SEC interpretive release further established a
multiprong test to decide whether a disclosure must be
made in the event that "a trend, demand, commitment,
event or uncertainty is known":

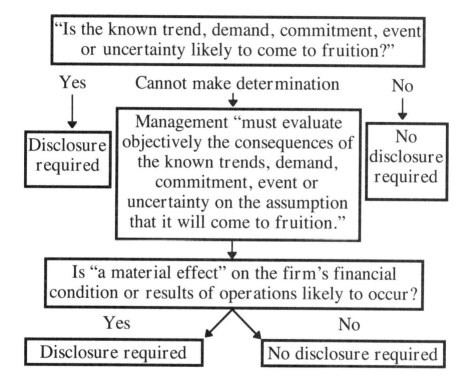

This flow diagram captures the essence of the nature
of the disclosure which the commission requires. Firms
must disclose all potential events unless they are not
likely to have a material effect. If past cases are any guide,
the SEC will bring enforcement actions against both individuals and their companies for not providing a meaningful
discussion of potential events.

The following excerpts from item 303 of Regulation
S-K and FRR 36 suggest the tone of the SEC in developing
guidance for an organization compiling its MD&A.

Liquidity:

"Identify any known trends or demands, commitments,
events or uncertainties that will result in or that are reasonably likely to result in the registrant's liquidity increasing or decreasing in any material way..."

Capital Resources:

"Describe any known material trends, favorable or unfavorable, in the registrant capital resources. Indicate any
expected material changes in the mix and relative cost of
such resources..."

Results of Operations:

"Describe any known trends or uncertainty that have had
or that the registrant reasonably expects will have a material favorable or unfavorable impact on net sales or revenues or income from continuing operations..."

If any of the following characteristics pertain to a
particular firm, they should be disclosed and addressed in
the MD&A:
1. The firm is likely to run out of cash.
2. The firm is seeking other sources of funding to prevent a
   cash shortage.
3. Chapter XI or Chapter VII is likely to be filed.

4. Discontinued operations or extraordinary gains or losses are likely to have a material effect on the firm's financials.
5. Reasons for any material change in the firm's revenues or expenses.
6. Any events (e.g. the loss of a principal customer), trends (e.g. increasing costs of raw materials which are likely to continue for several years), demands (e.g. increasing worldwide demand for the firm's key product), commitments (e.g. an agreement to externally contract a sales organization to carry out the bulk of the firm's sales), or uncertainties (e.g. the effect of the expiration of patent protection on the firm's major product line) which have a material effect on the firm's financials or operations.
7. Any materially disproportionate contribution to revenues, profitability and cash needs from any of the firm's industry segments.

Overall, the SEC requires a meaningful discussion of liquidity, capital resources and operating results to provide an understanding of its changes in financial condition and results of operations. To provide a clear assessment of the firm's operations, it also requires segment information where such information is appropriate to an understanding of the business.

MEASURING COMPANY HEALTH AND PERFORMANCE

Years ago, when corporations were first required to make financial statements available to shareholders, the intent was to provide an objective summary of corporate activity in dollar terms. Since that time, investors, creditors, business managers, and securities analysts have formulated methods – using financial statement data – to measure the soundness and performance of particular businesses. These include ratio and trend analyses. While the scope of this chapter does not permit a complete coverage of these subjects, the following overview is likely to be relevant to the practicing attorney. Throughout, we will use data drawn from financial statements of Harbor Systems Corporation to demonstrate methods of analysis.

RATIO ANALYSIS

Twenty-five hundred years ago, Greek sculptors discovered that the "ideal" human body conformed to certain proportions. The distance between the waist and the neckline, for example, should be a specific numerical fraction, or ratio, of the length of the entire body. The distance between the brow and the mouth should be a certain proportion of the length of the head. And so forth.

While no "ideal" measure exists for operating businesses, we do look to the proportions or "ratios" of many financial statement items to gain insight into business health and performance. These ratios fall into groups that measure liquidity, activity, leverage, and profitability.

Liquidity ratios. For a business, liquidity refers to its ability to meet maturing obligations, such as payments to creditors, taxes due to government, and repayments to lenders. In other words, "Can the firm pay its bills as they come due?" Firms that cannot, or that are barely able to pay current bills, or whose ability to pay bills would be jeopardized by a cyclical downturn in business are judged as poor risks by creditors and investors. As we will see later, the liquidity of a company at the time of its sale can be an issue in litigation.

Although liquidity can only be fully analyzed by a cash budget analysis, we can get a rough idea of a company's liquidity from the balance sheet ratio of current assets to current liabilities.

Reminder: Current assets are balance sheet items that can be turned into cash within a short time – usually one year. Generally, these are inventories, accounts receivable, marketable securities, and cash itself.

Current liabilities are obligations that must be paid in that same time frame. Generally, these are accounts payable, current portions of loans due, taxes due, and so forth.

When business people talk about "working capital," they should be referring to the difference between current assets and current liabilities. But it is surprising how many sophisticated people in business do not understand the concept of working capital. Many do not understand it at all while many others believe it is merely another way of describing cash! Generally, as a firm's sales increase, its working capital needs also increase. Inventories grow and so do receivables. A sales decrease typically results in a working capital decrease. In such a case, the firm will generally require less inventory and will fund fewer receivables. The issue of working capital for a firm is important because the funding of working capital requires cash. Increases in inventory must be paid for and similarly increases in accounts receivable must also be funded.

In the case of Harbor Systems, the *"current ratio"* is:

$$\boxed{\text{Current ratio}} = \frac{\text{Current assets}}{\text{Current liabilities}} = \frac{\$3.097 \text{ million}}{\$2.782 \text{ million}} = 1.11$$

This indicates that for every dollar of liabilities coming due during the coming year, the company has $1.11 available in the form of current assets. This thin margin would not be reassuring to anyone selling Harbor supplies on credit, or to a banker lending money to the company on a short-term basis. In many industries, current ratios greater than 2.0 are the norm.

A banker or business analyst looking at Harbor's current assets would notice that the bulk of these assets are represented by accounts receivable. "How likely is Harbor to collect on all of these receivables?" is the natural question. If more than $315 thousand of these are uncollectable, Harbor will have more current liabilities than current assets, which implies a reduced likelihood of meeting all its obligations as they become due.

Unlike Harbor, many companies have a significant proportion of their current assets tied up in inventory. In these cases, analysts often assess liquidity using the *quick ratio*:

$$\boxed{\text{Quick ratio}} = \frac{\text{Current assets} - \text{Inventory}}{\text{Current liabilities}}$$

The quick ratio removes inventory from the calculation, which is a good idea if the market value or the salability of a company's inventory is at all suspect.

Activity ratios. Activity ratios indicate how well a company employs its assets. Ineffective utilization of assets may result in the need for more funds, excessive interest expense and a correspondingly lower return on capital. Furthermore, low activity ratios or a deterioration in an activity ratio may indicate uncollectible accounts receivable or obsolete inventory or equipment.

A key activity ratio is *total asset turnover*, which measures the effectiveness of the company in utilizing its total assets. It indicates the level of sales the firm has achieved with the assets under its control. The ratio is defined as follows:

$$\boxed{\text{Total asset turnover}} = \frac{\text{Sales}}{\text{Total assets}}$$

For Harbor, total asset turnover is $\dfrac{\$6.135 \text{ million}}{\$3.997 \text{ million}} = 1.54$ times

The ratio indicates that Harbor has sales of $1.54 for every $1 of its assets. To understand whether this ratio reflects favorably or unfavorably on the firm, it is important to evaluate the ratio in context. Usually this is done by measuring ratios such as this one both over time and across similar firms. This way one is able to determine if there has been a deterioration over time or if the firm is a laggard in its industry. Indeed, later on in the chapter, such an analysis is described. While asset turnover measures the effectiveness of using all company assets, we may want to see how well a company is using specific assets: fixed assets, inventory, or accounts receivable. Fortunately, there are ratios for evaluating each.

$$\boxed{\text{Fixed asset turnover}} = \frac{\text{Sales}}{\text{Fixed assets}}$$

For Harbor, fixed asset turnover is $\dfrac{\$6,135,000}{\$298,269} = 20.6$ times

With a fixed asset turnover of 20, it is obviously not a capital intensive firm. Yet, to analyze the company in depth, one would compare this number to other firms in the industry as well as assess whether a trend exists in the ratio over the prior years.

$$\boxed{\text{Inventory turnover}} = \frac{\text{Cost of goods sold}}{\text{Inventory}}$$

For Harbor, inventory turnover is $\frac{\$3,069,144}{\$462,118} = 6.6$ times

While this ratio is based on end of the year inventory numbers, ratios of this type are often performed on numbers which are averages (e.g. average inventory during the year). This measure indicates how well the company is turning over its inventory. In addition, given that the cost of goods sold is related to the sales of the firm, low inventory turnover indicates that the firm carries too much inventory given its level of sales. Because inventory has to be financed, excess inventory typically affects the bottom line through increased interest expense. But the "best" level of inventory turnover is highly industry-dependent. For example, in some industries, such as groceries, normal turnover is extremely high, sometimes reaching more than 50-100 times a year.

Another important aspect of business effectiveness is the firm's ability to collect in a timely fashion from its clients. However, the accounts receivable collection period is also industry dependent. Utilities, with the threat of shut off, generally collect relatively quickly, while computer system companies often cannot collect until software runs bug-free. The *average collection period* is calculated as:

$$\boxed{\text{Average collection period}} = \frac{\text{Accounts receivable}}{\text{Sales/365 days}}$$

This measure indicates the average number of days that a company must wait to collect money earned through credit sales. As you can see, it requires two calculations: (1) annual credit sales (if not available, use "total sales" when virtually all sales are on credit) divided by 365 days; (2) divide that number into accounts receivable. Since such a high proportion of Harbor's current assets is tied up in receivables, any analysis of the company would dictate close scrutiny of this measure. If it were taking a long time to collect on these assets – and if the collection period were getting longer with each passing year – it would reflect poorly on business operations.

$$\text{Harbor's avg. collection pd.} = \frac{\$2.017 \ \text{million}}{\$6.135 \ \text{million} / 365} = 120 \ \text{days}$$

By just about anybody's definition, this would be described as "lousy" collection management. And even though systems firms have typically long collection periods, an average wait of 120 days for payment is worrisome.

Leverage ratios. The third basic type of financial ratio concerns leverage, or the use of borrowed money. Leverage ratios measure the relationship of funds provided by creditors to the investments made by owners. The use of borrowed funds by profitable companies improves the return on equity. However, borrowed funds increase the riskiness of the business and, if used in excessive amounts, can result in a financial disaster.

The *debt ratio* measures the total funds provided by creditors as a percentage of total assets; or:

$$\boxed{\text{Debt ratio}} = \frac{\text{Total debt}}{\text{Total assets}}$$

Total debt, as described here, is equal to total liabilities; essentially everything on the right hand side of the balance sheet with the exception of equity. Another way to calculate total debt is to simply subtract stockholders' equity from total assets. Debt occurs in many forms, including accounts payable, wages and benefits payable, income taxes payable, as well as bonds, notes and other borrowings from financial institutions and individuals.

$$\text{Harbor's debt ratio} = \frac{\$2.782 \text{ million}}{\$3.997 \text{ million}} = 69.6\%$$

In other words, almost $.70 out of each dollar of Harbor's assets are being financed by "OPM" – other people's money.

Note: Numerous leverage ratios are used by both attorneys and financial practitioners. For example, one of the most frequently used versions is the *debt-to-equity* ratio. But a caution here: the calculation depends on the user and how the user defines debt. A common definition of debt for this ratio includes only long-term debt. In other words, the ratio is often calculated by dividing long-term debt by the firm's equity (long-term debt/stockholders' equity). This ratio measures how much more (or less) the company uses debt relative to equity to fund its operations. Yet other definitions of the debt ratio exist and the attorney should be aware of the user's exact definition.

While the total debt ratio and the debt-to-equity ratio are based on balance sheet figures, the income statement provides us with another leverage indicator, the *times interest earned* ratio. It also provides insight into the ability of a company to meet its interest obligations. It is the ratio of earnings before interest and taxes (EBIT) to interest charges and it indicates the amount of funds available to cover scheduled interest payments.

$$\boxed{\text{Times interest earned}} = \frac{\text{EBIT}}{\text{Interest charges}}$$

Using Harbor System's income statement, we see that:

$$\text{Harbor's times interest earned ratio} = \frac{\$596{,}221}{\$227{,}720} = 2.6$$

There seems to be plenty of interest coverage here – assuming that the future is as rosy as the past. But as we will see in a later analysis, this ratio has dropped dramatically over the past year.

A similar ratio is the *fixed charge coverage* ratio, which recognizes that lease payments under long-term contracts are usually as mandatory as interest and principal payments on debt. The ratio is calculated as follows:

$$\boxed{\text{Fixed charge coverage ratio}} = \frac{\text{EBIT + Lease payments}}{\text{Interest charges + Lease payments}}$$

In the most recent year, Harbor Systems' annual lease payments were $114,000. Thus, its fixed charge coverage is:

$$\frac{\$596{,}221 + \$114{,}252}{\$227{,}720 + \$114{,}252} = 2.1 \text{ times}$$

This would tell anyone who was lending or leasing to Harbor Systems or investing in it that under current financial circumstances its earnings were sufficient to cover its fixed charges by a factor of two.

The final leverage ratio considered here is the *number of days payable*. This measures the average number of days that it takes the company to pay its suppliers. Like the average collection period, this ratio is calculated in two steps. First, divide annual purchases by 365 days to determine the average purchases per day (annual purchases/365 days). Then divide the accounts payable balance by the average purchases per day (accounts payable/average purchases per day) to determine the number of days of purchases that are still unpaid.

It is often difficult to determine the purchases of a firm. The income statement shows cost of goods sold, which for our friends at Harbor Systems not only includes purchases, but also direct labor for software development and overhead. Thus, often it is only possible to gain a rough idea as to whether or not a firm is becoming more or less dependent on its suppliers for funding its operations. However, by relating accounts payable to cost of goods sold [accounts payable ÷ (cost of goods sold/365)] and tracking this ratio over time, the analyst should be able to determine if the company is relying more or less on its suppliers for funding. This approximation makes sense as long as purchases remain a reasonably constant proportion of the cost of goods sold. Thus, when it is appropriate, we can use the approximation that:

$$\boxed{\text{Number of days payable}} = \frac{\text{Accounts payable}}{\text{Cost of goods sold}/365 \text{ days}}$$

For Harbor Systems, this is $\dfrac{\$504{,}517}{\$3{,}069{,}144/365} = 60$ days

Profitability ratios. Financial analysis provides a number of perspectives on profitability. Each improves our understanding of how well a particular company is performing. The first we consider is the firm's *gross margin.* It is a measure of the incremental profitability of each product sold and is measured as:

$$\boxed{\text{Gross margin}} = \frac{\text{Gross profit}}{\text{Sales}}$$

or

$$\boxed{\text{Gross margin}} = \frac{\text{Sales - Cost of goods sold}}{\text{Sales}}$$

For Harbor Systems, this is $\dfrac{\$3{,}065{,}856}{\$6{,}135{,}000} = 50\%$

In other words, at Harbor, 50% of the firm's sales revenues are used to meet its cost of goods sold (e.g. labor and material) and 50% of its sales revenues contribute to profit and are available to cover its other expenses (e.g. selling, general and administrative, interest), taxes and profits. We have been involved in cases where the gross margins have been as low as 8%. Unless there are unusual circumstances, 8% gross margins will rarely be sufficient to cover the firm's expenses, its taxes, and generate a positive profit. While the first profitability ratio is focused on the firm's gross profit, the second focuses on the firm's bottom line, its net income. It is the *"net profit margin,"* or net profit as a percentage of sales, which is derived by dividing after-tax earnings by revenues, or:

$$\boxed{\text{Profit margin}} = \frac{\text{Net income}}{\text{Sales}}$$

In Harbor Systems' case, this is $\dfrac{\$221,100}{\$6,135,000} = 3.6\%$

Like all other ratios, the 3.6% has the potential of being superb, just right, or poor, depending on the industry. For a supermarket chain, a low profit margin would not be surprising. But for a high-tech system company like Harbor, this would be a red flag that something was amiss. More on this later.

While the profit margin tells us the percentage of every dollar of sales that finds its way to the bottom line, it fails to recognize the degree of profitability the company is able to squeeze out of the assets employed in the business. To obtain this reading, analysts often use several other measures, the first being "*return on total assets*," which assesses profitability in terms of all assets employed – assets purchased with both borrowed money and equity. It is often measured in the following way:

$$\boxed{\text{Return on total assets}} = \frac{\text{Earnings before interest and taxes}}{\text{Total assets}}$$

Because of the lack of barriers to entry into the business and the resulting competition, companies operating in businesses requiring very little investment in fixed assets often have low profit margins on sales, but because of the low required investment, they earn very attractive returns on their invested funds. On the other hand, companies in very capital intensive businesses may earn low returns on assets, yet may have attractive profit margins on sales.

To enhance the comparability across companies within the same industry, it is useful to use the firm's operating earnings, which is defined as earnings before interest and taxes (EBIT). This makes it possible to consider only the firm's operations and to eliminate distortions due to both taxes and the manner in which the company is financed. Getting back to Harbor Systems we find that:

$$\text{Harbor's return on total assets is } \frac{\$596,221}{\$3,996,552} = 15\%$$

Our final profitability ratio has a tighter focus. Instead of looking at return on all assets, it measures the *return on common equity* (ROE), or the actual investment of shareholders. Here we divide after-tax earnings by the amount of common equity, as follows:

$$\boxed{\text{Return on equity}} = \frac{\text{Earnings after taxes}}{\text{Owners' equity}}$$

$$\text{For Harbor, return on equity is } \frac{\$221,100}{\$1,214,835} = 18.2\%$$

As you can probably surmise, as long as the return on assets is higher than the cost of borrowing, the more borrowed capital and the less owners' capital employed in the business, the higher the return on equity can be. This is the concept of "financial leverage," something we will examine in greater detail later in this book.

It is important to note that the return on equity we have just described is the firm's return on equity on the company's books. However, for a stockholder, the return on the equity she has earned in the stock market is typically the most relevant measure of performance. For example, if through dividends and price appreciation, the investor has generated $23,000 during the year on a

$100,000 investment, she was able to earn a 23% rate of return. It is this 23% return which the investor is able to bring to the bank, not the book return on equity measured earlier. Indeed, if the firm's historical performance has been poor, but because of a recent development its future prospects are bright, the book return on equity could be negative, yet the stock market-based ROE could have produced spectacular results for the investor. Both book and market return on equity have been popular measures on which to base the incentive compensation of senior managers. Yet, a number of companies – large and small – have begun employing a profitability performance metric called *economic value added*, or EVA. In its elemental form, EVA is a reflection of the firm's operating income less the product of its cost of capital and the capital employed by the firm:

> Economic value added = Operating income - (Cost of capital x Capital)

In the past, many of these same companies focused on return-on-equity. However, according to its adherents, EVA has the benefit of charging the earnings produced by managers with the cost of capital used to produce them. They argue that by both measuring and managing economic value added, one can create value more effectively than by using traditional performance measures.

As will be discussed in the cost of capital chapter, the cost of capital reflects both the cost of equity and the cost of debt. Therefore, as a behavioral tool, it makes decision-makers cognizant of the cost of both equity and borrowed capital. And since the firm's earnings are reduced by this cost, a manager whose compensation is tied to EVA would be expected to use capital with greater care. That, at least, is the hope.

Exhibit 1-5. Summary of Financial Ratios

Ratio	Formula
LIQUIDITY RATIOS	
Current ratio	$\dfrac{\text{Current assets}}{\text{Current liabilities}}$
Quick ratio	$\dfrac{\text{Current assets} - \text{Inventory}}{\text{Current liabilities}}$
ACTIVITY RATIOS	
Total asset turnover	$\dfrac{\text{Sales}}{\text{Total assets}}$
Fixed asset turnover	$\dfrac{\text{Sales}}{\text{Fixed assets}}$
Inventory turnover	$\dfrac{\text{Cost of goods sold}}{\text{Inventory}}$
Average collection period	$\dfrac{\text{Accounts receivable}}{\text{Sales}/365 \text{ days}}$
LEVERAGE RATIOS	
Debt ratio	$\dfrac{\text{Total debt}}{\text{Total assets}}$
Times interest earned	$\dfrac{\text{EBIT}}{\text{Interest expense}}$
Fixed charge coverage	$\dfrac{\text{EBIT} + \text{Lease payments}}{\text{Interest expense} + \text{Lease payments}}$
Days payable	$\dfrac{\text{Accounts payable}}{\text{Annual purchases}/365 \text{ days}}$
PROFITABILITY RATIOS	
Profit margin	$\dfrac{\text{Net income}}{\text{Sales}}$
Return on total assets	$\dfrac{\text{EBIT}}{\text{Total assets}}$
Return on equity	$\dfrac{\text{Net income}}{\text{Owners' equity}}$

GETTING BEHIND THE NUMBERS

So far, our study of financial statements has been purely a numbers game, showing you how the numbers appear in the statements and how specific ratios are calculated. The numbers and the ratios, however, are just the raw material for financial analysis. The rest involves perspective and judgment. To make the most of financial data, the analysts, creditors, lawyers or investors need to put them into perspective. Is Harbor Systems' 15% return on total assets good, bad, or average? Is the return improving or getting progressively worse? We can answer these questions by making use of industry ratios and using trend analysis.

INDUSTRY RATIOS

Financial analysts routinely compare one firm's financial ratios to those of its industry peer group. In the banking industry, for example, the industry's average return on total assets is a benchmark against which almost all banks are compared. In the case of Harbor Systems, we have already mentioned that its profit margin and average collection period ratios are red flags, strongly suggesting that we check equivalent ratios for its industry.

In some cases, industry ratios can also be misleading, since either (1) the categories into which companies are placed are very broad, or (2) so many companies have business units operating in more than one industry. For example, Hewlett-Packard is an electronics firm, but it has individual business units operating in software development, test and measurement instruments, high-end workstations, personal computers, and computer peripherals. It is well known that profit margins, cost structure and other financial measures are very different in the software and hardware industries. So which industry really defines Hewlett-Packard? In many cases, the most reliable approach to solving this problem is to develop ratios for the pool of a company's most direct competitors.

TREND ANALYSIS

Comparing the financial ratios of a particular company against those of its industry or direct competitors makes it possible to rank it in a pecking order of performance. However, this provides only a static sense of where the company stood when the numbers were obtained. We can expand that insight if we can determine the direction of a company's performance. For example, Harbor's profit margin is low, but has it been improving? Its current ratio is in the danger zone, but is this better or worse than past ratios? Are sales growing on a consistent basis? These are questions potentially answered through trend analysis.

The financial statements provided for Harbor Systems included three years of figures. We have used them to calculate several of the company's financial ratios for each of those years (Exhibit 1-6). This makes it possible, at a glance, to see both the level and direction of the company's health and performance.

On the positive side, Harbor Systems' sales are growing rapidly, at well over 50% per year. That is a trend that most companies would envy. Earnings before interest and taxes (EBIT) are growing at an even faster rate, practically doubling year-to-year, indicating that cost of goods and operating expenses are not getting out of hand. As indicated by Exhibit 1-6, Harbor Systems' rate of inventory turnover has declined from 8.6 in year 1 to 6.6 in year 3.

Exhibit 1-6. Selected Financial Ratios, 3 Years

Ratio	Yr1	Yr2	Yr3	Trend
Current ratio	3.9	1.7	1.1	Year-to-year deterioration
Return on total assets (%)	13.5%	16.2%	15%	Mixed signal
Inventory turn-over (times)	8.6	7.6	6.6	Year-to-year deterioration
Average collec-tion period (days)	120 days	120 days	120 days	Bad and not im-proving
Days payable	60 days	60 days	60 days	Stable
Debt ratio (%)	22.0%	48.7%	69.6%	Company is grow-ing more risky
Fixed charge coverage (times)	2.4	2.5	2.1	Recent drop
Profit as a percent of sales (%)	4.0%	4.2%	3.6%	Substandard and sinking

Another way to present this information is that in year 1 Harbor carried inventory for 42 days (365/8.6), while in year 3 this measure went up to 55 days.

The trend of other ratios is also disturbing. The company's low profit margin is not improving. Nor is its high average collection period. As the numbers indicate, Harbor pays its vendors' bills in 60 days (days payable) but collects its receivables in 120 days. The shortfall between cash collections and cash payments must be financed by borrowing, which is clear when we look at the cash flow statement (Exhibit 1-4). You will see there that in addition to the net income, the potential sources of cash flow are changes in working capital, investing activities, and financing activities. The first two are negative – uses of cash, while the only positive source is financing by lenders. These borrowings lead to an increase in Harbor's leveraged position, which in turn leads to an increase in interest expense, resulting in a decline in net income as a percentage of sales.

Other key ratios are also getting worse. Harbor's current ratio has dropped in each of the past three years to the point where it is at risk of having a "liquidity crunch." Meanwhile, increasing debt relative to owners' capital has increased the riskiness of the company to its lenders and raised the potential of failure for its owners. Perhaps as important, the dual effect of the company's liquidity problem and high debt burden means that its access to additional borrowing is surely limited, if not zero.

Companies with fast growing sales are typically short of cash. Those that do a good job of matching their payables with their receivables have a chance of financing their growth in an intelligent way. But this is often not the case. When a firm sells a system for $10,000, it gives the customer a credit on the full amount, while it gets credit from its vendor on only the material component of the $10,000 selling price. While this is the case with most manufacturing firms, other types of businesses might potentially have a negative working capital requirements. For example, supermarkets are typically paid for their sales in cash or checks. At the same time, they get credit from their food suppliers. Thus, for supermarkets, high growth usually does not create high working capital financing needs. Similarly, consider the typical airline. It does not hand you your ticket unless it is fully paid. If the ticket is sold through a travel agency, the airline also collects within a short period. In contrast, the airline gets credit from vendors such as food or fuel suppliers. Once again, growth might require financing more new planes, but not necessarily increased working capital needs. Most companies need some form of long-term capital – debt or added equity – as a foundation for growth. Harbor, unfor-

tunately, has done a poor job of matching payables and receivables, has no long-term debt, and only modest owner's
capital in the business.

FINANCIAL STATEMENT ANALYSIS: DETECTING EARLY WARNING SIGNALS

Financial ratios that are suspicious or heading in
the wrong direction on a year-to-year basis should be re-
garded as early warning signals for underlying business
problems. Obviously, there are numerous potential warning signals, each with a wide range of possible explana-
tions. The following are only examples of some of the
common symptoms and possible causes that merit investigation:

Symptom	Possible Causes
Collection period is increasing	The company may have changed its collection procedures and may not be billing as promptly.
	The industry may be heading for hard times.
	The products are not working properly and customers are delaying payment until problems are rectified.
Inventory turnover is slowing down	The firm's prices may be out of line with the rest of the industry.
	A new competitor is taking away market share.
	The firm's products are losing their competitive edge.
	Key sales people are leaving the firm.

Margins and profits are declining	The firm has lost key production and/or sales personnel.
	Products are improperly priced.
	The company has not effectively controlled the cost of custom jobs.
	The company has failed to take advantage of high margin opportunities.
	Salaries are growing too high.
	Competitors have brought more cost effective products to the market.
	Total sales have declined due to poor quality products.
	Aftermarket sales have declined because customers were not pleased with their original purchases.
	Products are being sold at reduced prices.
	A saturated market is putting downward pressure on prices.
Rate of new orders has declined	New sales personnel are not closing deals as rapidly as did their predecessors.
	Inadequate sales training.
	Market inroads by competitors.

Declining return on assets	More property has been purchased than was necessary to sustain growth. Inventory turnover is falling. The company has made capital outlays today for future growth tomorrow.
The current ratio is declining	Added short-term debt is being used to fund operations as cash flow worsens. Inventory level has declined. Payments to suppliers have slowed due to a tight cash position.
Total debt relative to equity has increased	Equity investors have not provided enough capital. The firm is focusing on return on equity and it therefore funds operations with added debt instead of added equity. Accounts receivable are being stretched beyond the firm's traditional collection period. Overhead is increasing and is being funded with borrowed money.
Sales are increasing at a slower rate than inflation	Products are less marketable due to advances in technology and design. The market has become saturated. New competitors have entered the market with superior products or services.

The company's cash position is extremely low	The company is growing too fast. Lenders are adverse to providing more funds due to the company's highly leveraged position. The company is too slow in collecting its receivables. Progress payments have been insufficient.
General and administrative expenses are increasing as a percentage of revenues	Sales have not kept pace with new hiring. The company has not implemented needed cost-cutting procedures. New product introductions have failed to meet expectations in sales.

THE DYNAMICS OF BUSINESS

Financial statements and other quantitative measures can tell us a great deal about a particular company. A skilled lawyer, working with no other information but several years of financial data, can develop amazing insight into a company that he or she has never even heard of.

But there is a side to business analysis that goes beyond the numbers. That other side is seldom quantifiable and represents the dynamics of a particular business: its people, markets, and competitors. Understanding the dynamics of a business requires attention to the quality of management, business strategy, the nature of competition, and even changing tastes and technology. In fact, the financials of a business are merely reflections of these other issues.

Competitive analysis. No analysis of a company is complete without attention to its markets and competitors. These, in many cases, explain many of the figures found in the financial statements. Harbor's 120 day collection period, for example, may be a function of a highly competitive situation, in which the only way to get a sale is to offer extremely generous credit terms. We need only observe the "0% financing, or no money down" schemes of Detroit's auto makers to understand how companies will offer financing perks when hard-pressed to move their merchandise.

One approach to understanding the nature of competition in a market is to develop a multi-dimensional matrix against which to "map" competitors. Exhibit 1-7 is a positioning map for Harbor Systems and its major competitors. The vertical dimension presents the geographic presence of these firms, while the horizontal dimension indicates the "value added" capabilities of the various competitors (low-level off-the-shelf service being one end, and highly customized, sophisticated architectural engineering systems on the other). A third dimension – the size of each firm, in terms of estimated sales – is represented by the size of each circle (competitors' names are represented by their initials). Positioning maps such as this one help the analyst to visualize where a company stands relative to its competitors and to identify both possible unserved markets and competitive threats.

Exhibit 1-7. Positioning Map for Harbor's Major
             Competitors

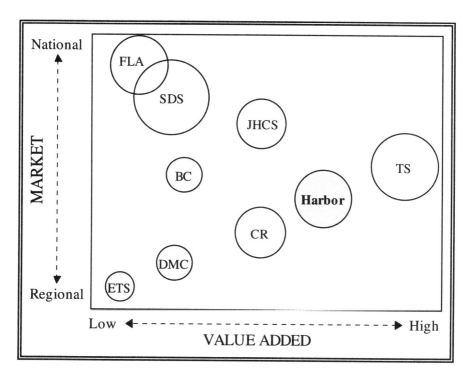

While the positioning map helps us understand the relative positions of directly competing companies, it tells us little about the other elements of a dynamic business situation, including: buyers, suppliers, potential entrants to the business, and even the challenge offered by substitute products or services. Exhibit 1-8 represents a framework for obtaining a broader view of business dynamics. This framework was originally developed by Professor Michael Porter in his book "Competitive Strategy" (the Free Press). You will notice that what we learned through the positioning map is largely confined to the central box.

Unfortunately for many companies, that center box is where they place all of their attention. Very often, the real threat is not one from their current competitors but from some unknown firm or one in an entirely different industry. Bankers learned this lesson in the hard way. One day they woke up to find much of their business captured by General Electric Credit, Merrill Lynch, Fidelity's mutual funds, and other non banks. Even suppliers can become competitors. Consider the evolution of the personal computer market. Initially, the hardware makers – IBM,

Exhibit 1-8. Dynamic Forces in Any Industry

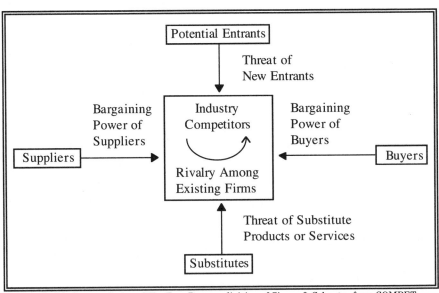

Reprinted with the permission of The Free Press, a division of Simon & Schuster from COMPET-ITIVE STRATEGY: Techniques for Analyzing Industries and Competitors by Michael E. Porter. Copyright © 1980 by The Free Press

Digital Equipment, Compaq, Packard Bell, Dell and others – occupied the center box. Later on, suppliers, such as Intel (the chip supplier) and Microsoft (the operating and applications software supplier), made the most money and determined the direction of the industry.

Quality of management. The quality of a company's management is probably the aspect of business dynamics which is most difficult to quantify, perhaps because good management is as much art as science. Still, the outside observer can probe for answers to key questions, such as:

- Does current management have experience with the types of challenges now facing the business? A CEO may have been a top performer when her company was at the small, entrepreneurial stage, but few entrepreneurs have the organizational skills to carry a company forward as it grows larger and becomes more complex.

- What are the company's goals? Has management developed a strategy to achieve them? Have they enlisted the support of other employees and given them the resources they need to be successful?

- Is management compensation closely aligned with the long-term success of the company? Many senior managers have princely salaries and golden parachutes to protect their futures. But they have little or no personal financial investment in their companies. They do well even when the companies they manage do poorly.

Chapter 2

The Time Value of Money

"We lost a major government contract because of their lousy components," complained the CEO of Navimetrics, Inc., an electronics manufacturer. His company had, indeed, been dropped from a multi-million dollar U.S. Navy contract. The cause was repeated failures in its airborne navigation devices, which, through analysis, were directly attributable to components sold to it by a supplier, AZ Circuitry.

The loss of the Navy contract was a financial blow to Navimetrics, and it looked to its supplier for damages. Because of quality assurances made to Navimetrics in its contract, AZ Circuitry thought it best to consider settlement. The only question was the extent of the damages. An outside accounting firm analyzed the situation and determined that Navimetrics would lose the following cash flows (in millions) over the five years of the Navy contract:

Year 1	Year 2	Year 3	Year 4	Year 5
$3	$5	$6	$4	$2

"That's $20 million in lost cash flows," said the Navimetrics CEO. "And we won't settle for a penny less."

The attorney for AZ Circuitry had another perspective. "We recognize our culpability in this matter, but a flat settlement now will have to be for less than $20 million, if only because of the time value of money."

This case underscores a common situation involving money and the timing of its receipt. For example, the purchase of an on-going business may involve the settlement of a current financial obligation by means of a series of payments made over several years. Still others aim to settle a present obligation with a single payment at some time in the future.

Each of these situations involves a fundamental concept of finance known as the time value of money. It is the same concept the mortgage banker uses when she figures the monthly payment on your home loan. It is also the same concept that makes it possible for you to determine how many dollars you must put away in a lump sum today to meet your son's college expenses ten years from now.

Of all the tools of modern finance, this is the most useful. And the mathematics of time and money can be applied to an almost endless set of financial problems, just a few of which are examined here.

This chapter explains the concept of the time value of money and demonstrates the use of its principal tools:

- the *future value of a present single sum*
- the *present value of a future single sum*
- the *future value of an annuity* (equal periodic payments)
- the *present value of an annuity*

These tools are extremely useful in cases involving subjects covered later in this book: damages, valuation and bankruptcy. Extensions of these tools are used in business every day: in capital budgeting decisions; in the analysis of the returns from current operations or investments; in calculating the growth rates for a business; and whenever mergers, acquisitions, or divestitures are contemplated. Such extensions include the following:

- net present value
- internal rate of return

These concepts are widely accepted and used daily in both the practice of corporate law and in litigation. Understanding them will help you communicate more with business clients and understand their financial concerns.

This chapter will show you how to perform time value calculations by means of a set of standard tables. This is the best way to learn. Solving the example problems with these tables will help you to appreciate the logic underlying time value concepts. Once you have the logic under your belt, we will explain how to do time value calculations using a financial calculator. These devices are inexpensive and easy to use.

THE FUTURE VALUE OF A PRESENT SINGLE SUM

Everyone understands that money left in an interest-paying savings account will compound over time. This is probably the most commonplace example of the time value of money at work. *Compounding* means that the principal amount in the account and the interest earned periodically in the account will both earn interest. It is this compounding effect that makes savings accounts grow exponentially instead of at a linear rate, accelerating into an upward curve of growing value, as shown in Exhibit 2-1.

As the exhibit demonstrates, the higher the rate of interest paid, the greater the growth in value. So, if you put $100 into an account at 5% interest compounded annually, that value will increase over the first ten years to approximately $163. At 10% interest, that final value is a much larger amount – approximately $259. (The flat line indicates "simple interest," interest that does not compound over time.)

Another point worth noting is that the frequency of compounding also affects the outcome. For example, a 10% savings account that compounds monthly will produce a larger amount over the years than the same account that compounds annually. Our example in Exhibit 2-1 grew from $100 to $259 by compounding annually at 10% over

Exhibit 2-1. The Power of Compound Growth

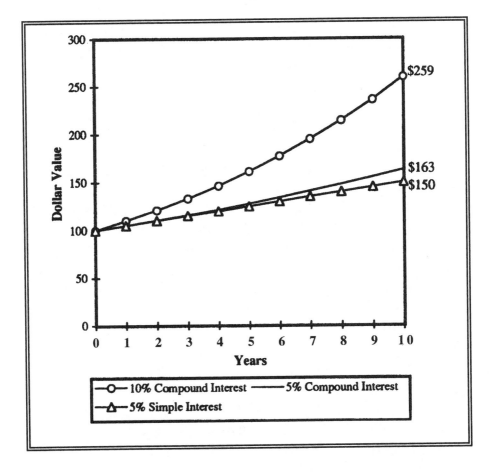

ten years.   Had this same account compounded on a monthly basis, its value at the end of the tenth year would have been around $271.

> The more frequent the compounding, the greater the end-of-period accumulated value.

As the concept of compound interest sinks in, think about Client McDonald, a man who has suffered $100,000 in damages in a business transaction that happened five years ago. Assuming that his current claim is valid, we need to determine what his claim should be today.   We know intuitively that it should be more than $100,000. Had McDonald been given the money when the damage occurred, he could have invested the $100,000 in some interest-bearing security – perhaps in a five-year Treasury note at 5%.   Therefore, what we are looking for in a settlement is the future value of $100,000 compounded annually at 5% over a period of five years.

But how much would that future value be?   We can calculate future value directly using the standard future value table. Here, we are trying to determine the future value of a present single sum.

The future value of a present single sum is what a current sum will increase to over a certain period of time at some compounding rate.

To calculate future value, let us frame the problem within a format that can be used as we move to more complex cases.   Here we have what is called a "present value" (PV), the compounding rate (i), the number of compounding periods (n), and a quantity we hope to determine – the future value (FV). Consider a $1 initial deposit compounded at a 10% interest rate.

$$PV = \$1 \quad\quad i = 10\% \quad\quad\quad n = 1 \quad\quad\quad FV = ?$$

If we multiply the PV times the annual i we get the amount by which our PV will increase in one period:

$$PV \times i = \$1 \times .10 = \$0.10$$

Adding this $0.10 of earnings to our original $1 gives us a FV of $1.10. If we left our interest and original sum in an account to compound at the same rate for another year, we would have:

$$\$1.10 \times .10 = \$\ 0.11 \text{ in earned interest;}$$
$$\$1.10 + .11 = \$1.21$$

So, the FV of $1 compounded at 10% for two years is $1.21.

Now look at Exhibit 2-2, "Future Value of $1." The compounding periods (n) are arrayed horizontally across the top, and the different rates of return (here from 1% - 20%) are arrayed vertically down the left-hand side. The numbers in the table are what we call "future value interest factors" or FVIFs. As you can see from the intersection for 1 period at 10%, our calculation of the FV of our $1 is $1.10. For 2 periods it is $1.21. You can use this table to determine the future value of any other sum for any given period. For practice, we can use it to find the future value of the $100,000 claimed by Client McDonald.

Exhibit   2-2

FUTURE VALUE OF $1

INTEREST RATE	YEARS									
	1	2	3	4	5	6	7	8	9	10
1%	$1.0100	$1.0201	$1.0303	$1.0406	$1.0510	$1.0615	$1.0721	$1.0829	$1.0937	$1.1046
2%	$1.0200	$1.0404	$1.0612	$1.0824	$1.1041	$1.1262	$1.1487	$1.1717	$1.1951	$1.2190
3%	$1.0300	$1.0609	$1.0927	$1.1255	$1.1593	$1.1941	$1.2299	$1.2668	$1.3048	$1.3439
4%	$1.0400	$1.0816	$1.1249	$1.1699	$1.2167	$1.2653	$1.3159	$1.3686	$1.4233	$1.4802
5%	$1.0500	$1.1025	$1.1576	$1.2155	$1.2763	$1.3401	$1.4071	$1.4775	$1.5513	$1.6289
6%	$1.0600	$1.1236	$1.1910	$1.2625	$1.3382	$1.4185	$1.5036	$1.5938	$1.6895	$1.7908
7%	$1.0700	$1.1449	$1.2250	$1.3108	$1.4026	$1.5007	$1.6058	$1.7182	$1.8385	$1.9672
8%	$1.0800	$1.1664	$1.2597	$1.3605	$1.4693	$1.5869	$1.7138	$1.8509	$1.9990	$2.1589
9%	$1.0900	$1.1881	$1.2950	$1.4116	$1.5386	$1.6771	$1.8280	$1.9926	$2.1719	$2.3674
10%	$1.1000	$1.2100	$1.3310	$1.4641	$1.6105	$1.7716	$1.9487	$2.1436	$2.3579	$2.5937
11%	$1.1100	$1.2321	$1.3676	$1.5181	$1.6851	$1.8704	$2.0762	$2.3045	$2.5580	$2.8394
12%	$1.1200	$1.2544	$1.4049	$1.5735	$1.7623	$1.9738	$2.2107	$2.4760	$2.7731	$3.1058
13%	$1.1300	$1.2769	$1.4429	$1.6305	$1.8424	$2.0820	$2.3526	$2.6584	$3.0040	$3.3946
14%	$1.1400	$1.2996	$1.4815	$1.6890	$1.9254	$2.1950	$2.5023	$2.8526	$3.2519	$3.7072
15%	$1.1500	$1.3225	$1.5209	$1.7490	$2.0114	$2.3131	$2.6600	$3.0590	$3.5179	$4.0456
16%	$1.1600	$1.3456	$1.5609	$1.8106	$2.1003	$2.4364	$2.8262	$3.2784	$3.8030	$4.4114
17%	$1.1700	$1.3689	$1.6016	$1.8739	$2.1924	$2.5652	$3.0012	$3.5115	$4.1084	$4.8068
18%	$1.1800	$1.3924	$1.6430	$1.9388	$2.2878	$2.6996	$3.1855	$3.7589	$4.4355	$5.2338
19%	$1.1900	$1.4161	$1.6852	$2.0053	$2.3864	$2.8398	$3.3793	$4.0214	$4.7854	$5.6947
20%	$1.2000	$1.4400	$1.7280	$2.0736	$2.4883	$2.9860	$3.5832	$4.2998	$5.1598	$6.1917

How much will McDonald's $100,000 have grown to over a period of five years at a compounding rate of 5%? To find the answer, go to Exhibit 2-2, and see where the 5 year row intersects the 5% column. There, the FVIF is 1.2763. This means that every dollar invested at 5% will be worth $1.2763 at the end of 5 years. In McDonald's case:

$$\$100,000 \times 1.2763 = \$127,630$$

Note: Everything we have described thus far is based upon the mathematics of finance and is universally accepted. The one thing you should always be concerned with when using this or other time value tools is the rate at which the compounding will occur. If you sought a settlement of McDonald's case using the 5% given here, the other side would ask, "Why 5%? Why not 3%." Over long periods of time, a small change in the compounding rate magnifies the future value enormously. We will discuss this issue later in the chapter.

  And remember, the frequency of the compounding period will also affect the future value.

THE PRESENT VALUE OF A FUTURE SINGLE SUM

Present value is generally defined as the current worth of an amount to be received in the future. This concept is the "flip side" of the future value concept described above.

  To understand present value of a future single sum, consider this situation: Your client has already purchased a business and must have exactly $1,276,300 on hand as a final payment in five years time. You suggest that he put enough money into a 5% certificate of deposit today (a present value) to meet this obligation five years in the future. The question is: what is "enough money?"

Here we need to determine what present value compounded at 5% over 5 full years will give us a future value of $1,276,300. Graphically, we could present this as shown in Exhibit 2-3. In this and subsequent graphic presentations of time value, arrows pointing upward represent positive cash flows; those pointing downward are negative cash flows – losses, deposits, or payments.

Exhibit 2-3. Calculating the Present Value of a Future Sum

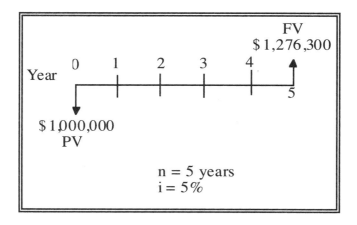

If you have not already recognized it, this is just the reverse of Client McDonald's case described earlier. In that case we knew the present value, the interest rate, and the number of compounding periods. We had to solve for future value. Here we know the future value, but not the present value. This is "backwards compounding," or, in the language of finance, a process of "*discounting*" a future sum to a present value.

Again, tables make it possible to solve for the present value directly. (See Exhibit 2-4, the present value of

$1.) To use the present value table, simply find the intersection of period 5 and 5%. The number at that intersection – 0.7835 – is the present value interest factor (PVIF); it indicates how many dollars must be invested now in order to compound to a value of $1 in five years.

Now, to determine the amount your client should place in a five year CD today to meet his payment obligation in five years, we multiply the FV times the present value interest factor, or

$$\$1,276,300 \text{ x } 0.7835 = \$1,000,000$$

THE FUTURE VALUE OF AN ANNUITY DUE

Strictly defined, an annuity is a sequence of equal annual payments. In 1475, France's Louis XI ended the Hundred Years War and rid his nation of foreign troops by promising England's Henry VI an *"annuity"* of 50,000 Crowns. In 1860, the Sioux Indians went on the warpath in the Minnesota territory because the government failed to pay them their "annuity" of cash, meat, and blankets. Today, state-run lotteries employ the concept of the annuity to pay out sums won by contest winners. "Tonight's Megadollars winner will receive $1 million paid out as $50,000 per year over the next 20 years!" (As we will soon see, this is a clever ploy on the part of lottery commissions to pay out less than what most ticket buyers think they will receive.) In legal cases, structured settlements – a series of periodic payments – are another example of the annuity concept.

Exhibit 2-4

PRESENT VALUE OF $1

INTEREST RATE	YEARS									
	1	2	3	4	5	6	7	8	9	10
1%	$0.9901	$0.9803	$0.9706	$0.9610	$0.9515	$0.9420	$0.9327	$0.9235	$0.9143	$0.9053
2%	$0.9804	$0.9612	$0.9423	$0.9238	$0.9057	$0.8880	$0.8706	$0.8535	$0.8368	$0.8203
3%	$0.9709	$0.9426	$0.9151	$0.8885	$0.8626	$0.8375	$0.8131	$0.7894	$0.7664	$0.7441
4%	$0.9615	$0.9246	$0.8890	$0.8548	$0.8219	$0.7903	$0.7599	$0.7307	$0.7026	$0.6756
5%	$0.9524	$0.9070	$0.8638	$0.8227	$0.7835	$0.7462	$0.7107	$0.6768	$0.6446	$0.6139
6%	$0.9434	$0.8900	$0.8396	$0.7921	$0.7473	$0.7050	$0.6651	$0.6274	$0.5919	$0.5584
7%	$0.9346	$0.8734	$0.8163	$0.7629	$0.7130	$0.6663	$0.6227	$0.5820	$0.5439	$0.5083
8%	$0.9259	$0.8573	$0.7938	$0.7350	$0.6806	$0.6302	$0.5835	$0.5403	$0.5002	$0.4632
9%	$0.9174	$0.8417	$0.7722	$0.7084	$0.6499	$0.5963	$0.5470	$0.5019	$0.4604	$0.4224
10%	$0.9091	$0.8264	$0.7513	$0.6830	$0.6209	$0.5645	$0.5132	$0.4665	$0.4241	$0.3855
11%	$0.9009	$0.8116	$0.7312	$0.6587	$0.5935	$0.5346	$0.4817	$0.4339	$0.3909	$0.3522
12%	$0.8929	$0.7972	$0.7118	$0.6355	$0.5674	$0.5066	$0.4523	$0.4039	$0.3606	$0.3220
13%	$0.8850	$0.7831	$0.6931	$0.6133	$0.5428	$0.4803	$0.4251	$0.3762	$0.3329	$0.2946
14%	$0.8772	$0.7695	$0.6750	$0.5921	$0.5194	$0.4556	$0.3996	$0.3506	$0.3075	$0.2697
15%	$0.8696	$0.7561	$0.6575	$0.5718	$0.4972	$0.4323	$0.3759	$0.3269	$0.2843	$0.2472
16%	$0.8621	$0.7432	$0.6407	$0.5523	$0.4761	$0.4104	$0.3538	$0.3050	$0.2630	$0.2267
17%	$0.8547	$0.7305	$0.6244	$0.5337	$0.4561	$0.3898	$0.3332	$0.2848	$0.2434	$0.2080
18%	$0.8475	$0.7182	$0.6086	$0.5158	$0.4371	$0.3704	$0.3139	$0.2660	$0.2255	$0.1911
19%	$0.8403	$0.7062	$0.5934	$0.4987	$0.4190	$0.3521	$0.2959	$0.2487	$0.2090	$0.1756
20%	$0.8333	$0.6944	$0.5787	$0.4823	$0.4019	$0.3349	$0.2791	$0.2326	$0.1938	$0.1615

In finance, the concept of an annuity is not strictly bound to annual payments. It simply refers to a periodic stream of equal-sized payments. Nor is it restricted to regular outgoing payments. It can also refer to equal periodic deposits made to a pool of money, as in a retirement plan. For example, if you are making $10,000 annual contributions to a savings or retirement plan, you are participating in an annuity arrangement.

Earlier, we illustrated the PV and FV concepts with a simple diagram. In Exhibit 2-5 we do the same for the annuity. Here, the downward arrows indicate annual amounts paid into an account at the beginning of each period, which, with compounding, creates some future value. The upward arrow indicates the amount received at the end of the final period.

Exhibit 2-5. Calculating the Future Value of an Annuity

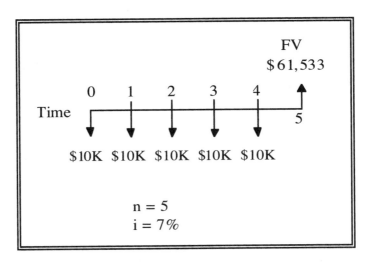

If you are putting $10,000 into your Keogh account at the beginning of each year for a period of five years at 7% interest, your Keogh will have a value of $61,533 at the end of five full years.

Here we have what is called an *"annuity due,"* i.e., a series of equal payments (PMTs) made at the beginning of each compounding period (n) at a specified rate (i). The job here is to figure the FV for all of these PMTs. (Be aware that there is an "ordinary annuity," which is a PMT made at the end of each period.)

There are two ways to determine the FV for a stream of annuity due PMTs. The first is more tedious, and is offered here by way of illustration, as it helps us see into the problem more clearly. Here consider Exhibit 2-6, which lays out the series of $10,000 annual PMTs over five years.

Exhibit 2-6. Calculating the Future Value of an Annuity
            Due – Period by Period

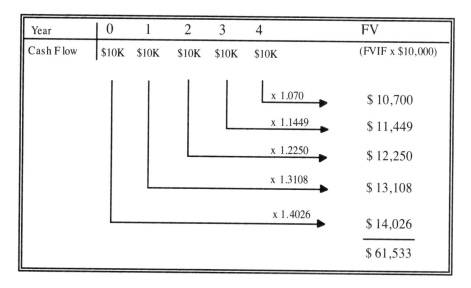

Year	0	1	2	3	4		FV
Cash Flow	$10K	$10K	$10K	$10K	$10K		(FVIF x $10,000)
					x 1.070		$ 10,700
					x 1.1449		$ 11,449
					x 1.2250		$ 12,250
					x 1.3108		$ 13,108
					x 1.4026		$ 14,026
							$ 61,533

In this exhibit we rely on a method already learned: figuring the FV of $1. In this case we find the FVIFs for $1 at 7% for 5, 4, 3, 2, and 1 compounding periods, multiply each of those factors times $10,000, and determine the FV of each Keogh plan contribution. For example, the first of those annual $10,000 investments compounds for five full years; the last compounds for only one full year. Summing these individual FVs, we obtain the future value of the entire series of Keogh contributions, which is the total of all the $10,000 contributions plus interest.

The second approach to solving this problem is much simpler, involving the use of Exhibit 2-7, the Future Value of an Annuity Due.

This table is only of value in those cases in which the amount of the annuity PMT is always the same, and when the PMT is made at the *beginning of* each period. Since both conditions prevail in our Keogh example, we extract the future value interest factor for five periods at 7% – 6.1533 – and multiply it by the $10,000 PMT:

$10,000 x 6.1533 = $61,533

Both methods produce the same answer. So why did we bother with the first explanation, in which we laboriously figured the FV of each PMT, then summed the results? One good reason is to provide a method of analysis for those typical situations in which the PMTs are of different amounts. For example, if you had made contributions of five different amounts to your Keogh, the first method would have estimated its total FV. The table method for calculating the FV of an annuity due would have been of no use.

THE FUTURE VALUE OF AN ORDINARY ANNUITY

In the parlance of finance, an *"ordinary annuity"* is one where the payments are received at the end of each com-

Exhibit 2-7

FUTURE VALUE OF AN ANNUITY DUE

INTEREST RATE	YEARS									
	1	2	3	4	5	6	7	8	9	10
1%	$1.0100	$2.0301	$3.0604	$4.1010	$5.1520	$6.2135	$7.2857	$8.3685	$9.4622	$10.5668
2%	$1.0200	$2.0604	$3.1216	$4.2040	$5.3081	$6.4343	$7.5830	$8.7546	$9.9497	$11.1687
3%	$1.0300	$2.0909	$3.1836	$4.3091	$5.4684	$6.6625	$7.8923	$9.1591	$10.4639	$11.8078
4%	$1.0400	$2.1216	$3.2465	$4.4163	$5.6330	$6.8983	$8.2142	$9.5828	$11.0061	$12.4864
5%	$1.0500	$2.1525	$3.3101	$4.5256	$5.8019	$7.1420	$8.5491	$10.0266	$11.5779	$13.2068
6%	$1.0600	$2.1836	$3.3746	$4.6371	$5.9753	$7.3938	$8.8975	$10.4913	$12.1808	$13.9716
7%	$1.0700	$2.2149	$3.4399	$4.7507	$6.1533	$7.6540	$9.2598	$10.9780	$12.8164	$14.7836
8%	$1.0800	$2.2464	$3.5061	$4.8666	$6.3359	$7.9228	$9.6366	$11.4876	$13.4866	$15.6455
9%	$1.0900	$2.2781	$3.5731	$4.9847	$6.5233	$8.2004	$10.0285	$12.0210	$14.1929	$16.5603
10%	$1.1000	$2.3100	$3.6410	$5.1051	$6.7156	$8.4872	$10.4359	$12.5795	$14.9374	$17.5312
11%	$1.1100	$2.3421	$3.7097	$5.2278	$6.9129	$8.7833	$10.8594	$13.1640	$15.7220	$18.5614
12%	$1.1200	$2.3744	$3.7793	$5.3528	$7.1152	$9.0890	$11.2997	$13.7757	$16.5487	$19.6546
13%	$1.1300	$2.4069	$3.8498	$5.4803	$7.3227	$9.4047	$11.7573	$14.4157	$17.4197	$20.8143
14%	$1.1400	$2.4396	$3.9211	$5.6101	$7.5355	$9.7305	$12.2328	$15.0853	$18.3373	$22.0445
15%	$1.1500	$2.4725	$3.9934	$5.7424	$7.7537	$10.0668	$12.7268	$15.7858	$19.3037	$23.3493
16%	$1.1600	$2.5056	$4.0665	$5.8771	$7.9775	$10.4139	$13.2401	$16.5185	$20.3215	$24.7329
17%	$1.1700	$2.5389	$4.1405	$6.0144	$8.2068	$10.7720	$13.7733	$17.2847	$21.3931	$26.1999
18%	$1.1800	$2.5724	$4.2154	$6.1542	$8.4420	$11.1415	$14.3270	$18.0859	$22.5213	$27.7551
19%	$1.1900	$2.6061	$4.2913	$6.2966	$8.6830	$11.5227	$14.9020	$18.9234	$23.7089	$29.4035
20%	$1.2000	$2.6400	$4.3680	$6.4416	$8.9299	$11.9159	$15.4991	$19.7989	$24.9587	$31.1504

Exhibit   2-8

FUTURE VALUE OF AN ORDINARY ANNUITY

INTEREST RATE	1	2	3	4	5	6	7	8	9	10
					YEARS					
1%	$1.0000	$2.0100	$3.0301	$4.0604	$5.1010	$6.1520	$7.2135	$8.2857	$9.3685	$10.4622
2%	$1.0000	$2.0200	$3.0604	$4.1216	$5.2040	$6.3081	$7.4343	$8.5830	$9.7546	$10.9497
3%	$1.0000	$2.0300	$3.0909	$4.1836	$5.3091	$6.4684	$7.6625	$8.8923	$10.1591	$11.4639
4%	$1.0000	$2.0400	$3.1216	$4.2465	$5.4163	$6.6330	$7.8983	$9.2142	$10.5828	$12.0061
5%	$1.0000	$2.0500	$3.1525	$4.3101	$5.5256	$6.8019	$8.1420	$9.5491	$11.0266	$12.5779
6%	$1.0000	$2.0600	$3.1836	$4.3746	$5.6371	$6.9753	$8.3938	$9.8975	$11.4913	$13.1808
7%	$1.0000	$2.0700	$3.2149	$4.4399	$5.7507	$7.1533	$8.6540	$10.2598	$11.9780	$13.8164
8%	$1.0000	$2.0800	$3.2464	$4.5061	$5.8666	$7.3359	$8.9228	$10.6366	$12.4876	$14.4866
9%	$1.0000	$2.0900	$3.2781	$4.5731	$5.9847	$7.5233	$9.2004	$11.0285	$13.0210	$15.1929
10%	$1.0000	$2.1000	$3.3100	$4.6410	$6.1051	$7.7156	$9.4872	$11.4359	$13.5795	$15.9374
11%	$1.0000	$2.1100	$3.3421	$4.7097	$6.2278	$7.9129	$9.7833	$11.8594	$14.1640	$16.7220
12%	$1.0000	$2.1200	$3.3744	$4.7793	$6.3528	$8.1152	$10.0890	$12.2997	$14.7757	$17.5487
13%	$1.0000	$2.1300	$3.4069	$4.8498	$6.4803	$8.3227	$10.4047	$12.7573	$15.4157	$18.4197
14%	$1.0000	$2.1400	$3.4396	$4.9211	$6.6101	$8.5355	$10.7305	$13.2328	$16.0853	$19.3373
15%	$1.0000	$2.1500	$3.4725	$4.9934	$6.7424	$8.7537	$11.0668	$13.7268	$16.7858	$20.3037
16%	$1.0000	$2.1600	$3.5056	$5.0665	$6.8771	$8.9775	$11.4139	$14.2401	$17.5185	$21.3215
17%	$1.0000	$2.1700	$3.5389	$5.1405	$7.0144	$9.2068	$11.7720	$14.7733	$18.2847	$22.3931
18%	$1.0000	$2.1800	$3.5724	$5.2154	$7.1542	$9.4420	$12.1415	$15.3270	$19.0859	$23.5213
19%	$1.0000	$2.1900	$3.6061	$5.2913	$7.2966	$9.6830	$12.5227	$15.9020	$19.9234	$24.7089
20%	$1.0000	$2.2000	$3.6400	$5.3680	$7.4416	$9.9299	$12.9159	$16.4991	$20.7989	$25.9587

pounding period. Consider what would happen if your annual $10,000 Keogh contributions were made at the end of each period instead of at the beginning. The calculation would produce a slightly different FV for the same stream of PMTs at the same interest rate. To determine that FV we use Exhibit 2-8, the Future Value of an Ordinary Annuity.

In this case, we look at the table for the future value interest factor for 5 periods at 7%. This number is 5.7507. It is what $1 invested at the end of each of five periods at 7% will be worth at the end of 5 years. Multiplying that factor by the PMT of $10,000, we obtain $57,507.

Lesson: If you want to maximize the future value of an annuity, make sure that the cash inflows are made at the *beginning* of each period. For example, if a settlement requires that the other party contributes $100,000 each year to an account on behalf of your client, ask that those payments be made at the beginning of the year. Over a five year period at 7%, for example, such a "minor" timing difference would result in an additional $40,255 for your client – a sizable difference.

THE PRESENT VALUE OF AN ORDINARY ANNUITY

Your client, Mr. Jones, is arranging the sale of his dry cleaning business to a potential buyer, Ms. Appleby. Jones is holding out for a single payment upon closing of the sale, whereas Appleby and her attorney are trying to negotiate a series of three $100,000 payments, the first payable one year after the closing, and the remaining payments every year thereafter. "I'd rather have all the money up-front," Jones grouses, figuring that he could invest the money in Treasury notes at 6% interest.

During the negotiations between Jones and Appleby, a second potential buyer appears. "I'll pay you $240,000 for the business on closing," says the second buyer. Now Jones is in a dilemma. Appleby is willing to pay a total of $300,000 over time, but the second buyer is offering $240,000 right now. Based entirely upon the monetary arrangements in these two offers, which is better for Jones?

This is a typical time value problem in business. Someone is faced with differentiating between money now and money received as payments or receipts over different time periods. In some cases, as here, there are a series of equal periodic receipts (PMTs) – in effect, an annuity; in other cases, the amounts may differ and they may appear at irregular intervals. Ms. Appleby's offer, thankfully, is simple, and we can find the present value of that offer by finding, and summing, the present value of the three payments.

Exhibit 2-4 shown earlier, the Present Value of $1, can be used to solve this problem. Quite simply, we find the present value interest factor for $1 received one year in the future discounted, in this case, by 6% and multiply it by the first $100,000 payment. Exhibit 2-9 shows this and the treatment of the second and third year payments as well.

The present value of the three future payments sums to $267,300. Assuming that Jones does not need all of his cash right away, this is superior to the $240,000 "on closing" offer of the second buyer.

Exhibit 2-9. Finding the Present Value of Ms. Appleby's
          Offer

PV $100,000 x PVIF		Time 1	Time 2	Time 3
$94,340	◄—— 0.9434 —— $100K			
$89,000	◄—— 0.8900 ——————— $100K			
$83,960	◄—— 0.8396 ———————————— $100K			
$267,300				

Notice one thing about this exhibit. The present
value of individual payments "deteriorates" rapidly as
their actual receipt is further and further in the future.
Discounted at 6%, a $100,000 payment received at the end
of the 10th year would have a present value of only
$55,839!

Time is not the only factor to deteriorate the present
value of future payments. Higher discount rates (i), have
the same effect. Discounted at 12%, the same $100,000
received at the end of year 10 has a PV of only $32,197!

The method just shown for determining the present
value of a stream of future sums can accommodate "messy"
cash flow situations – i.e., those with different sized sums
received at any interval, regular or otherwise. As we will
see shortly, and in our chapter on valuation, most business
problems fall into this "messy" category. Very rarely, we
encounter one like Ms. Appleby's offer, in which an equal
stream of periodic payments is involved. On those occa-
sions, we can use Exhibit 2-10, Present Value of An Ordinary Annuity.

Here we simply find the present value interest factor
for 6% over 3 periods, or 2.6730, and multiply it times the

Exhibit   2-10

PRESENT VALUE OF AN ORDINARY ANNUITY

INTEREST RATE	YEARS									
	1	2	3	4	5	6	7	8	9	10
1%	$0.9901	$1.9704	$2.9410	$3.9020	$4.8534	$5.7955	$6.7282	$7.6517	$8.5660	$9.4713
2%	$0.9804	$1.9416	$2.8839	$3.8077	$4.7135	$5.6014	$6.4720	$7.3255	$8.1622	$8.9826
3%	$0.9709	$1.9135	$2.8286	$3.7171	$4.5797	$5.4172	$6.2303	$7.0197	$7.7861	$8.5302
4%	$0.9615	$1.8861	$2.7751	$3.6299	$4.4518	$5.2421	$6.0021	$6.7327	$7.4353	$8.1109
5%	$0.9524	$1.8594	$2.7232	$3.5460	$4.3295	$5.0757	$5.7864	$6.4632	$7.1078	$7.7217
6%	$0.9434	$1.8334	$2.6730	$3.4651	$4.2124	$4.9173	$5.5824	$6.2098	$6.8017	$7.3601
7%	$0.9346	$1.8080	$2.6243	$3.3872	$4.1002	$4.7665	$5.3893	$5.9713	$6.5152	$7.0236
8%	$0.9259	$1.7833	$2.5771	$3.3121	$3.9927	$4.6229	$5.2064	$5.7466	$6.2469	$6.7101
9%	$0.9174	$1.7591	$2.5313	$3.2397	$3.8897	$4.4859	$5.0330	$5.5348	$5.9952	$6.4177
10%	$0.9091	$1.7355	$2.4869	$3.1699	$3.7908	$4.3553	$4.8684	$5.3349	$5.7590	$6.1446
11%	$0.9009	$1.7125	$2.4437	$3.1024	$3.6959	$4.2305	$4.7122	$5.1461	$5.5370	$5.8892
12%	$0.8929	$1.6901	$2.4018	$3.0373	$3.6048	$4.1114	$4.5638	$4.9676	$5.3282	$5.6502
13%	$0.8850	$1.6681	$2.3612	$2.9745	$3.5172	$3.9975	$4.4226	$4.7988	$5.1317	$5.4262
14%	$0.8772	$1.6467	$2.3216	$2.9137	$3.4331	$3.8887	$4.2883	$4.6389	$4.9464	$5.2161
15%	$0.8696	$1.6257	$2.2832	$2.8550	$3.3522	$3.7845	$4.1604	$4.4873	$4.7716	$5.0188
16%	$0.8621	$1.6052	$2.2459	$2.7982	$3.2743	$3.6847	$4.0386	$4.3436	$4.6065	$4.8332
17%	$0.8547	$1.5852	$2.2096	$2.7432	$3.1993	$3.5892	$3.9224	$4.2072	$4.4506	$4.6586
18%	$0.8475	$1.5656	$2.1743	$2.6901	$3.1272	$3.4976	$3.8115	$4.0776	$4.3030	$4.4941
19%	$0.8403	$1.5465	$2.1399	$2.6386	$3.0576	$3.4098	$3.7057	$3.9544	$4.1633	$4.3389
20%	$0.8333	$1.5278	$2.1065	$2.5887	$2.9906	$3.3255	$3.6046	$3.8372	$4.0310	$4.1925

annual payment of $100,000 to find our answer: $267,300, the same answer which was obtained through the other method.

Earlier in this chapter we said that we would show you how state lottery commissions follow the P.T. Barnum dictum to "Never give a sucker an even break." For years, these commissions have been getting away with a scam that any state's attorney would have nailed had the perpetrator been a private company. The scam is this: promise lottery winners millions of dollars but really pay them only 50-55 percent of what you promise.

Here's how it works: Mrs. Oldfield, a poor widow and habitual lottery player, actually wins a $1 million prize. The lottery commission agrees to pay her that million in 20 annual installments of $50,000 before taxes (20 x $50,000 = $1 million). Unfortunately, the present value of those payments discounted by 7% (the approximate rate at which she could have safely invested the sum) is a mere $529,700. This is the approximate amount that the commission will actually place into an interest-bearing account to meet its obligations to Mrs. Oldfield over the next 20 years. Exhibit 2-11 tells the tale. Some lotteries start the

Exhibit 2-11. The Present Value of a $1 Million Lottery Win Paid Over a 20-year Period

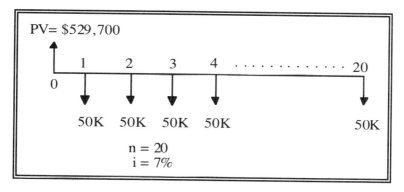

20-year payout stream in period 0. If this is the case, the value of the lottery winnings is greater, namely $566,780, due to the earlier receipt of the funds. Such a payment stream is often referred to as an annuity due and is described in the next section.

THE PRESENT VALUE OF AN ANNUITY DUE

The last of the standard tools we'll show you is the present value of an annuity due. An annuity due is a series of equal periodic payments, each received at the beginning of a compounding period – i.e., the first payment occurs now. Leasing agreements involve annuity due payment. When you borrow, you typically make monthly payments at the end of a period; when you lease, these payments are made at the beginning of the month.

Consider the example of a law firm that leases a networked computer system for $20,000 per year over the course of 5 years, with each year's lease payment due at the beginning of the year. Here we are trying to calculate the PV of an annuity due. And, of course, there is a handy table for making the calculation – shown in Exhibit 2-12. In this case we use an annual after-tax interest rate of 6%.

Looking at Exhibit 2-12, we see that the PV interest factor for an annuity due for 5 years at 6% is 4.4651. In other words, if you discounted a $1 payment made at the beginning of 5 years by 6%, its present value would be $4.4651. Simply multiply this figure times the actual annual lease payment to find the PV of the 5 annuity payments.

$$PV = \$20,000 \times 4.4651$$
$$= \$89,302$$

Exhibit   2-12

PRESENT VALUE OF AN ANNUITY DUE

INTEREST RATE	YEARS									
	1	2	3	4	5	6	7	8	9	10
1%	$1.0000	$1.9901	$2.9704	$3.9410	$4.9020	$5.8534	$6.7955	$7.7282	$8.6517	$9.5660
2%	$1.0000	$1.9804	$2.9416	$3.8839	$4.8077	$5.7135	$6.6014	$7.4720	$8.3255	$9.1622
3%	$1.0000	$1.9709	$2.9135	$3.8286	$4.7171	$5.5797	$6.4172	$7.2303	$8.0197	$8.7861
4%	$1.0000	$1.9615	$2.8861	$3.7751	$4.6299	$5.4518	$6.2421	$7.0021	$7.7327	$8.4353
5%	$1.0000	$1.9524	$2.8594	$3.7232	$4.5460	$5.3295	$6.0757	$6.7864	$7.4632	$8.1078
6%	$1.0000	$1.9434	$2.8334	$3.6730	$4.4651	$5.2124	$5.9173	$6.5824	$7.2098	$7.8017
7%	$1.0000	$1.9346	$2.8080	$3.6243	$4.3872	$5.1002	$5.7665	$6.3893	$6.9713	$7.5152
8%	$1.0000	$1.9259	$2.7833	$3.5771	$4.3121	$4.9927	$5.6229	$6.2064	$6.7466	$7.2469
9%	$1.0000	$1.9174	$2.7591	$3.5313	$4.2397	$4.8897	$5.4859	$6.0330	$6.5348	$6.9952
10%	$1.0000	$1.9091	$2.7355	$3.4869	$4.1699	$4.7908	$5.3553	$5.8684	$6.3349	$6.7590
11%	$1.0000	$1.9009	$2.7125	$3.4437	$4.1024	$4.6959	$5.2305	$5.7122	$6.1461	$6.5370
12%	$1.0000	$1.8929	$2.6901	$3.4018	$4.0373	$4.6048	$5.1114	$5.5638	$5.9676	$6.3282
13%	$1.0000	$1.8850	$2.6681	$3.3612	$3.9745	$4.5172	$4.9975	$5.4226	$5.7988	$6.1317
14%	$1.0000	$1.8772	$2.6467	$3.3216	$3.9137	$4.4331	$4.8887	$5.2883	$5.6389	$5.9464
15%	$1.0000	$1.8696	$2.6257	$3.2832	$3.8550	$4.3522	$4.7845	$5.1604	$5.4873	$5.7716
16%	$1.0000	$1.8621	$2.6052	$3.2459	$3.7982	$4.2743	$4.6847	$5.0386	$5.3436	$5.6065
17%	$1.0000	$1.8547	$2.5852	$3.2096	$3.7432	$4.1993	$4.5892	$4.9224	$5.2072	$5.4506
18%	$1.0000	$1.8475	$2.5656	$3.1743	$3.6901	$4.1272	$4.4976	$4.8115	$5.0776	$5.3030
19%	$1.0000	$1.8403	$2.5465	$3.1399	$3.6386	$4.0576	$4.4098	$4.7057	$4.9544	$5.1633
20%	$1.0000	$1.8333	$2.5278	$3.1065	$3.5887	$3.9906	$4.3255	$4.6046	$4.8372	$5.0310

"Why would I want to know this?" you might ask.

One good reason is to determine whether it is better for your law firm to lease or buy the computer system in question. Assuming 1) that the computer system will be obsolete and have no resale value after five years, and 2) that the cost of operating and maintaining the system will be the same whether it is bought or leased, you could compare the $89,302 to the cost of buying the system outright. If the purchase price less any tax benefits associated with depreciation is less than this present value figure, it may be better to simply buy it.

"But if I bought this machine, instead of leasing it," you object, "I'd forgo the opportunity to earn interest on that money."

And you would be right. Economics 101 comes drifting back. There is an *opportunity cost* to the "buy" alternative. The company could have invested the purchase price in some interest-bearing security; or it could have invested it in current operations, producing revenues and profits over the years to come.

This brings us back to the 6% rate we used to discount those annuity payments. Why did we pick this number? When finance people select a discount rate in a leasing problem, they select a rate that reflects one of the following:

1. the after-tax rate they could expect to earn on an investment of comparable risk, or
2. the after-tax rate they could expect to pay for funds to make an investment of comparable risk.

These are straightforward. The first is used when the firm has the funds available to make this or alternative investments. The second is used when the firm must obtain external funds to invest in the asset. Both relate to risk and return. The higher the risk – i.e., the more uncertain the future outcome – the higher the rate of return the investor or business person will expect to receive if funds are available for investment. Moreover, if funds are obtained externally, the riskier the stream of cash flows to be financed, the greater the discount rate employed. Obviously, the riskier the venture, the higher the return a provider of funds will require. For relatively certain cash flows, such as lease payments, the discount rate used is frequently the after-tax cost of borrowing. For more risky cash flows, such as the salvage value of the equipment, the discount rate is often the cost of capital. So, when forced to select a discount rate for a time value problem, financial professionals choose one that is commensurate with the level of risk associated with the cash flows of the venture.

The cost of capital of the business is complex and is dealt with in a separate section of this book. Suffice it to say here that the capital that finances a business's assets and operations has a cost to the business. Capital borrowed from bankers, bondholders, and other sources has a very explicit cost: the interest rate on those borrowed funds. Shareholders also provide capital to the firm, and they, too, expect a rate of return. It is the weighted average of these different rates that determines the cost of capital for a company.

TIME VALUE SOLUTIONS MADE EASY: USING A FINANCIAL CALCULATOR

The methods shown above represent the basic time value calculations. As you have probably noticed, each involves the same elements – sometimes calculating from the present to the future; sometimes from the future to the present. Variations of these methods are available to cover more complex situations: when compounding periods (n) are months instead of years; when a stream of cash flows contains *negative* as well as positive values; when cash flows are of different sizes; and so forth. All of these situations, however, contain these factors, either as knowns or unknowns:

Present value: PV
Future value: FV
Payments: PMT
Compounding rate (or discount rate): i
Number of compounding periods: n

Every time value problem contains these factors. There may be instances in which either PMTs, PV, or FV may be zero, but there are five factors nevertheless. If you know four of them, you can solve for the fifth. Solving time value problems for PMT, i, or n is much more difficult without a calculator. And these problems arise in legal situations all the time. A simple financial calculator, however, can solve them for you quickly and accurately. Most of these calculators are priced under $100. Each is preprogrammed to solve for the unknown once the known factors are entered. Most have very similar routines for entering and computing time value of money situations, and come with instruction books that explain the particular steps to take in solving a variety of problems.

To understand how these calculators work, consider the "generic" model below. Like other models, it has special buttons for each of the time value factors. This calculator also has buttons that you use to tell the machine whether a payment is being made at the beginning or end of a compounding period (it makes a difference).

To solve time value problems with this device, let's go back to Client McDonald, who needed to find the future value of single sum. His situation can be described by the following chart:

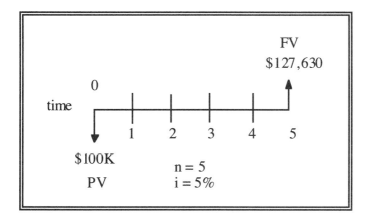

Here we need to calculate the future value of $100,000 if we put it away today at 5% interest compounded annually for five full years. With the calculator, this is simple. After clearing the financial registers, enter $100,000 (changing its sign to negative because it is a cash outflow) and punch the PV button. Then enter 5 and punch the n button. This is the number of compounding periods. Then enter 5 for the interest rate and punch the i button. Finally, press the "compute" or "calculate" button followed by pressing the FV button. The FV, $127,630, will appear in the display.

As you can see, just as with the table solution method, the answer is $127,630. But wasn't that simpler?

Now let us try to solve some typical problems that the table method will not help you to solve – that is, unless you have many hours and several blackboards available! Only MBA students should ever be forced to do this type of hand labor!

Illustration 1: *Determining the periodic payment (PMT)*. Your client agrees to buy a small business for $250,000. The seller agrees to finance the purchase at an annual rate of 12% over a period of 4 years. What monthly payment (PMT) will pay off the loan and interest?

Solution: Because you are looking for the monthly payment, you need to consider the monthly interest rate and the number of monthly periods in 4 years. (Always begin your solution by clearing the calculator's memory.)

PV = -$250,000 (most calculators will have you tag this figure with a negative sign)
i = 12/12 = 1 (the monthly rate)
n = 4 x 12 = 48 (the number of monthly payments in 4 years)
PMT = ? To determine the monthly payment, press PMT, or "compute" PMT, depending on your particular calculator.

The answer is $6,583.46.

Illustration 2: *Determining the compounding rate (i)*. Your client is awarded a settlement of $1 million. For liquidity reasons, the other side offers to pay $350,000 at the end of each of the next three years. What is the compounding rate that reduces these payments to the present value of $1 million? In other words, what is the interest rate your client is earning by trading a current payment of $1 million for three future annual payments of $350,000 each?

Solution:
PV = -$1,000,000
PMT = $350,000
n = 3
i = ? To determine the compounding rate in this problem, press i.

The answer is 2.48%. This is the rate of return your cli-ent is being asked to accept to solve the other side's li-quidity problem.

Illustration 3: *Determining the number of compounding pe-riods (n)*. A business owner intends to invest $100,000 each month at 8% interest with the goal of creating an $8 million pool of cash for future expansion. How many months will it take her to reach this goal?

Solution:
PMT = -$100,000
i = 8/12 = .67 (the monthly interest rate)
FV = $8,000,000
n = ? To determine the number of periods (months) the
owner will need to reach her goal, press n.

The answer is 64.3 months.

A more complex problem: *The Creditor Committee deci-sion*. Lawyers who deal with bankruptcies are familiar with the operations of committees formed to represent the interest of creditors in bankruptcy proceedings. In many cases, these committees must answer the question: are the creditors better off if the company is liquidated now or if it continues to operate? In other words, are they better off if the company is dead or alive?

In these cases, creditor committees need to compare the company's estimated current liquidation value to the present value of a stream of estimated future cash flows. This is one of those "messy" problems we described earlier, and knowing how to solve it will help you to see a very common situation through different eyes. Consider this example.

Capital Realty Company is bankrupt. A committee of creditors has done two things: it has estimated the current liquidation value to be $6 million; and it has also estimated that new management could operate the company in a way that Capital Realty would produce the following cash flows (in $ millions) from operations over the next five years:

Year 1	Year 2	Year 3	Year 4	Year 5
$0	$1	$2	$2	$3

Further, an accounting firm has estimated that the value of Capital Realty at the end of the fifth year would be $2 million. We can present these cash flows graphically:

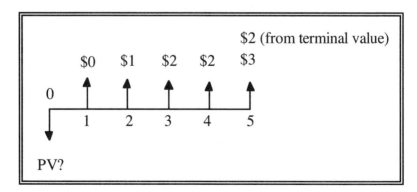

If you were on the creditors committee, you would want to know if the current $6 million liquidation value was more or less than the present value of these future cash flows. Before you can solve the problem, however, you must do one thing: determine the compounding, or discount, rate (i).

Choosing the discount rate. In most of our examples, we have used the current interest rate on bank CDs or Treasury securities – "safe money" investment rates – for i. In the world of finance, however, we typically use a rate commensurate with the riskiness of the cash flows we are discounting. In effect, we use a discount rate that reflects the rate of return we would expect to make on an investment with a comparable risk. The higher the risk, the higher the rate of return we would expect to make.

In the example just given, we already know that Capital Realty is shaky – it is in bankruptcy; so how solid are these projected cash flows? After considering the facts of this case, prudence would dictate that we use a high discount rate: for example, an annual rate of 16%.

To solve our problem with Capital Realty Company, we will find the PV of each cash flow in turn, and then add them up following these steps:

1. Clear the memory and the calculator's display according to the manufacturer's instructions.
2. Enter 16% as the value for i, the discount rate.
3. We're now ready to enter the first cash flow. Since the one at the end of the first year is $0, we will ignore it. The next cash flow appears at the end of Year 2. Enter 2 as the value for n, the number of compounding periods.
4. Enter $1 million and press FV.

5. Press PV. This will give you $743,162.90. (With most calculators, this will have a negative sign.). Either write this number down or store it in memory.

We need to find the PV of each future cash flow in this manner. As you do so, i stays the same at 16%, but n increases year by year.

Once you get to the fifth year, total the estimated cash flow of $3 million with the estimated $2 million net sale value of Capital Realty's assets ($3 million + $2 million) and find its PV. As you would expect, i = 16%; n = 5; and FV = $5,000,000.

In the end we find this solution:

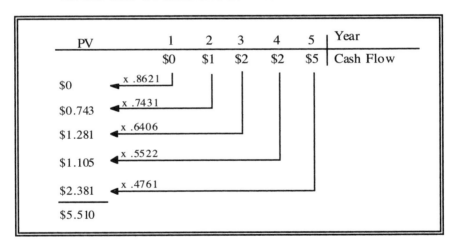

Thus, the present value of Capital Realty's estimated cash flows is $5.51 million, somewhat less than its current liquidating value. The credit committee now has information upon which to make a better decision.

THE NET PRESENT VALUE

Many business and legal situations involve series of cash flows involving one or more negative cash flows. A typical business problem might involve the purchase of a business – a negative cash flow – followed by a stream of positive cash flows from ongoing business operations. Attorneys who deal with valuations or mergers and acquisitions confront these on a regular basis. We can alter the previous problem slightly to create the following scenario:

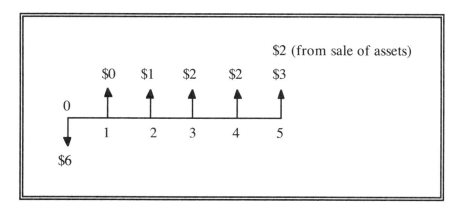

Here, we have indicated an up-front (time 0) payment of $6 million for the purchase of a company with the indicated cash flows. The purchaser will want to know: "If I pay $6 million for this company, and if my required rate of return is 16%, what is the net present value of the investment?"

The net present value (NPV) is the present value of a project's or acquisition's future cash flows less the cost of the project or acquisition. In other words, the NPV is the present value of all the cash inflows minus the present value of all the cash outflows. NPV is used by decision makers to determine whether or not they should go ahead with an investment. If the NPV is positive, it indicates that they are expected to earn a rate of return higher than their cost of capital. NPV is also used to compare one investment alternative to another. If one has a higher NPV, it is the superior choice.

With this in mind, the problem presented above is solved as follows:

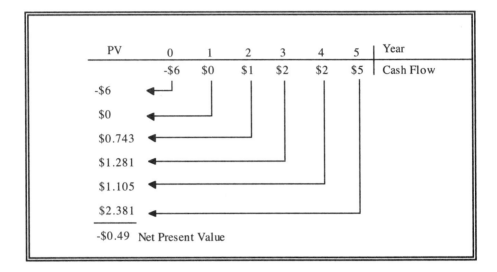

In this case, the net present value is negative, meaning that at the purchase price of $6 million the investment does not quite produce the 16% return required by the buyer. The present value of the future cash inflows is $490,000 short of the $6 million purchase price. It is so close to zero, however, that a $500,000 lower purchase price would swing the NPV outcome.

INTERNAL RATE OF RETURN

One question you may have about the situation shown above is "What rate of return would this set of cash flows produce for the buyer?" Supposing that the business is purchased for $6 million and produces the stream of cash flows described, what rate of return does this actually represent. We determine that return by solving for what the financial professionals call the *internal rate of return*, or IRR. The IRR is the *discount rate* that produces a net present value of zero. In other words, it is the discount rate (i) that exactly equates the present value of future cash flows to the purchase price.

Finding IRR for an uneven stream of cash flows (i.e., a nonannuity) without the benefit of a financial calculator is a major chore, but not difficult if you follow the instructions in your calculator's manual. Most devices have cash flow keys: CF_0 and CF_j, for example. Typically, you input the numbers in order, beginning with the first cash flow. In our example above, CF_0 is -6 million. You then enter 0 as CF_1, 1 as CF_2, and so forth, being sure to get the order right.

Having done this, you press the key labeled "IRR" to get the solution. In our example, the IRR is 13.52%.

Note: The mathematics of IRR has an implicit assumption that all cash flows received will be reinvested at the same rate as the IRR. In the example given, it assumes that the cash flows received in years 2, 3, 4, and 5 are not spent, but reinvested at a rate of 13.52%.

Another Illustration: *Finding the rate of return.* Not all IRR problems include a negative cash flow. In some cases you simply need to find the rate of return earned on some investment over time based upon its starting and ending values. Here is a fairly typical problem found in damage cases involving securities.

At the very beginning of Year 1, High-Growth Portfolio Management approached the pension manager of QRS, Inc., claiming that it could produce an excellent return on its funds with minimal risk by creating a diverse portfolio of stable, blue-chip stocks. This plan seemed sufficiently plausible that the pension manager gave High-Growth $10 million of its pension fund to manage. No other funds were involved.

Over the course of three years, account statements made it appear that High-Growth was following the plan and producing results. Every year, the value of the portfolio increased. By the middle of the fourth year, the account value was $14 million. Then the portfolio's value began dropping. By the end of the fourth year, its value stood at $11.2 million. Upon investigation, QRS, Inc. discovered that the money managers were playing a risky game using index options. It sued High-Growth on the basis that it had deliberately deviated from the low-risk strategy it had promised and, as a result, had produced an inferior return.

The first step in determining the damages is to determine the actual rate of return earned on the portfolio over the course of exactly four years. Graphically, we can show the situation as:

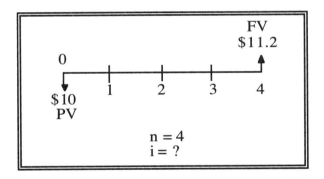

Here we know the PV, the FV, and n. What we are looking for is the i that will compound $10 million to a value of $11.2 million over the course of 4 full years.

Fortunately, our calculator makes this easy. Just follow these steps.

PV = -10 million
FV = 11.2 million

n = 4

i = ? Press i to get the solution of 2.87%

The answer is the annual compound rate of return on the portfolio. It also indicates the discount rate that would be necessary to bring a future stream of cash flows back to its present value. In the very simple case just given, 2.87% is the discount rate that makes the $11.2 million received at the end of year 4 equal to the present value of $10 million.

As you can see through these examples, once you have correctly structured the problem, solving them with a financial calculator is relatively easy. Most financial calculators have excellent manuals containing all sorts of time value problems, how to structure them, and which keystroke to use in reaching the right solutions. If you have such a manual, take the time to master the material it contains. We will provide still more time value applications in subsequent chapters, and you will see the power of time value principles in legal situations involving damages, business valuations, securities, bankruptcies, and mergers and acquisitions.

Chapter 3

Securities

Many cases involving securities are litigated each year. Some are claims against investment advisors and fiduciaries involving alleged violation of "the prudent man rule" or from alleged portfolio mismanagement. Others arise from broker/customer disputes; the most prevalent of these involve "churning" – i.e., excessive trading of a client's account to generate brokerage commissions – and the sale of "unsuitable" investments to customers. Unsuitability cases involve disputes in which a customer alleges that a stockbroker or investment advisor deliberately induced an investment or strategy that was inappropriate, given the investor's financial situation, investment goals, or aversion to risk. Cases of rogue stockbrokers convincing elderly pensioners to put their life savings into oil and gas drilling partnerships and other illiquid and risky ventures are all too familiar, and are typical of unsuitability cases.

Still other litigation arises from the failure to observe regulations regarding disclosure of material company information. Disclosure cases typically occur when material information about a firm or its officers is not made available to investors in a timely or public manner, as prescribed by securities authorities. Very often, the complaint is that information about the riskiness of the firm's securities was deliberately withheld.

Risk and return are central to every investment decision. So it should not be surprising that legal disputes involving securities frequently involve these concepts. The heart of the typical case is the measurement of risk and return. In particular, the question of how much return is necessary for a given amount of risk is frequently the core of the case.

This chapter examines the concepts of risk and return, how each is measured, and how they are bound together. The "science" that relates to risk and return is among the most fertile in modern finance, and its principles provide the theoretical foundation upon which much of the industry of investment management is currently based. Some of those principles are laid out in the following pages. Understanding them will improve your insights into many of the legal disputes involving securities.

Many investors and corporations have sought to manage risk through specially designed financial instruments, which generally fall under the term "derivatives." We also present a section on the use of derivatives to manage risk.

RISK

Risk is a normal component of life – our companion when we commute to work each morning, when we allow the doctor to vaccinate us against disease, and when we make virtually all business decisions. Risk is so much a part of life that we usually give it little thought. Nor do we give much thought to the fact that we accept these risks as part of a tradeoff in which we expect some benefit. The daily commute to work contains a small statistical probability that we will be killed or injured, yet we accept this minor risk because of the benefit of rapid transportation.

In layman terms, risk is often defined as the chance of loss. In the investment field, however, risk means the uncertainty of return. For example, if an investor puts $50,000 into three month T-bills, there is very little uncertainty as to the return. An investment in a newly formed biotech firm, however, is most likely a highly uncertain undertaking. It may be a bonanza for the investors, or it may produce a substantial loss. It is the uncertainty of returns that provides our measure of risk.

In the investment world, uncertainty and the potential for loss go with the territory. We generally categorize risk as either systematic or unsystematic. Systematic risk is the uncertainty of return inherent in the "system" of which a particular security is a part. A share of Hewlett-Packard common stock, for example, is part of a larger "system", which includes the stock market, the economy as a whole, and the moods of investors in general – none of which are under the control of Hewlett-Parkard's managers. If the Federal Reserve tightens the money supply, or if war breaks out in the Middle East, the stock market will probably go down across the board, taking Hewlett-Packard shares with it.

Debt securities, such as bonds, are likewise subject to systematic risk. If prevailing interest rates rise, the market value of City of Chicago bonds will fall, even though that city's ability to meet its obligations to bondholders is unimpaired.

Virtually all investments are subject to some form of systematic risk. And, as we will see shortly, this form of risk cannot be avoided without avoiding investments entirely.

Some forms of risk, however, are directly associated with or uniquely particular to individual securities. These are called unsystematic risks. In the case of Hewlett-Packard stock just mentioned, unsystematic risk stems from the chance that the company may lose a major product liability lawsuit, that it will make a major investment in a product line that fails in the marketplace, or that it will be eclipsed by its competitors. These uncertainties are independent of factors affecting the mood of investors, other industries, and so forth. They are particular to the company itself. Total risk is the sum of these two forms of risk:

> Total risk = Systematic risk + Unsystematic risk

MEASURING RISK

How can we determine if a security or a portfolio is more risky than another? Is there an objective measure capable of telling us that 'Stock A is twice as risky as Stock B'? The answer to these questions is "yes." In fact, there are several measures, with the two commonly used metrics of risk being the standard deviation and the beta.

Standard deviation. Standard deviation is a statistical measure of volatility – it captures the ups and downs of investment returns in a single number. Basically, it measures the total risk of the security. Its calculation is more involved than what we need here. For our purposes, suffice it to say that:

> Standard deviation is a statistical measure that considers the distance of all data points from the average of all the points.

Confused? To appreciate this measure of volatility, consider the stocks of Play Toy, Inc. and Basic Foods, Inc. in Exhibit 3-1. The average market price of each stock over the period of a year is exactly the same: $15. But just looking at the exhibit, it is clear that Play Toy, being in the toy business, is much more volatile. It has a higher stan-

Exhibit 3-1. Volatility of Play Toy, Inc. and Basic
Foods, Inc.

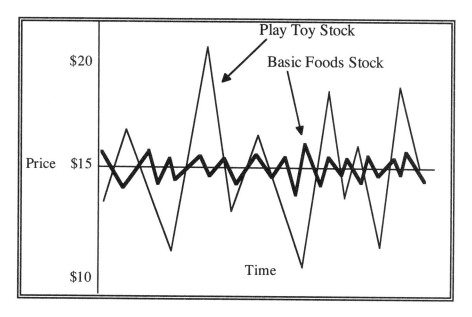

dard deviation. Therefore, Play Toy stock is riskier than
Basic Foods stock.

Beta coefficient. Another valuable measure of risk is
the beta coefficient. While the standard deviation measures the total risk of a security, the beta is a measure of a
security's systematic risk. It provides us with a measure of
a security's risk relative to the market as a whole (often
represented by the Standard & Poor's 500 stocks).

Financial scholars have noted that some stocks are
more sensitive to the general market movements – both up
and down – than others. Thus, when the market as a whole
goes up 10%, the stock of Play Toy goes up 20%. When the
market goes down 10%, Play Toy drops by 20%. By applying a statistical technique called regression analysis to
past rates of return on an individual stock or a portfolio
versus rates of return on the market as a whole, we are

able to derive a single number that describes the volatility of that stock or portfolio relative to the overall market. This measure is called the stock's (or the portfolio's) beta.

Exhibit 3-2 demonstrates the application of regression analysis to the return of a particular stock relative to the return on the market. Though generally scattered, we can see that the points in the exhibit (the return of the stock relative to the market for a number of periods) tend to move in the same general direction as market returns. As the return on the market increases, so does the return on the stock. The line in the exhibit, called the characteristic line, is determined through regression analysis. It represents the "best fit" of a straight line through the scattered data points. The slope of the line (the "rise over the run") is the stock's beta.

In this particular case, the slope of the line is 0.9, which implies that, in general, the historical return on the stock typically increases and decreases at a slightly slower rate than the market return. A similar interpretation is that this stock is slightly less volatile than the market. Depending on the methodology used to calculate the characteristic line, the beta may differ. Not infrequently in securities litigation, the expected return figures presented to the court are contested and dependent on the methodology used to determine the security's beta.

In beta analysis, the market as a whole has a beta of 1.0. Securities with betas greater than 1.0, such as airline stocks, have above-average volatility (risk) relative to the market; stocks with betas less than 1.0, such as food company stocks, are less volatile than the market as a whole. A stock with a beta of 1.0 would be expected to move in same direction and at the same rate of change as the market. A stock with a beta of 2.0 would be expected to be 100% more volatile than the market. Thus, if Play Toy

Exhibit 3-2. The Characteristic Line

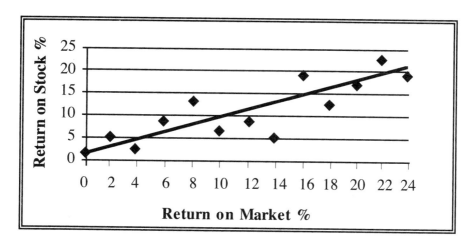

stock had a beta of 2.0 and the S&P 500 market index dropped 10%, we would expect Play Toy stock to drop some 20%. The betas of a number of well-known company stocks are shown in Exhibit 3-3.

Applying this reasoning to Intel stock, whose beta is 1.35, we would expect that a 5% decline in the overall market would result in a 6.75% decline in Intel's market price (5% x 1.35 = 6.75%). Obviously, the same relative volatility also works when the market goes up rather than down.

Some stocks, though very few, have negative betas, meaning that they move in the opposite direction to the overall market. For example, a stock with a beta of -1.0 would be expected to move in the opposite direction to the market, and to the same degree. Thus, if the market rose 10%, a security with a beta of -1.0 would be expected to drop by 10%.

Exhibit 3-3. Company Betas

Deere	1.40
Citicorp	1.35
Intel	1.35
Wal-Mart Stores	1.25
General Motors	1.15
Delta Airline	1.15
Disney	1.15
Procter & Gamble	1.10
McDonald's	1.05
IBM	1.00
Exxon	0.60
Homestake Mining	0.25

Stock betas are calculated on a regular basis and made available by information service companies such as Standard & Poor's, Moody's Investment Services, and Value Line.

A Caution On Betas: Betas are calculated from *past* movements of the market and individual stocks. Thus, a stock's beta is based on history that may or may not repeat itself in the future.   To some degree, betas may change over time.   Also, there is no "standard" way to calculate betas; each information service uses a slightly different method.   The result is that betas may differ slightly depending upon who is performing the calculations.

REDUCING RISK THROUGH DIVERSIFICATION

It is widely understood that a portion of total risk – namely the unsystematic risk – can be reduced through diversification. Diversification is the process of adding securities to a portfolio such that the overall volatility of the portfolio is reduced. Diversification has its greatest effect when these securities are weakly correlated with each other. By weakly correlated, we mean that the returns of particular securities do not move in lock-step with each other.

All stocks are correlated to a certain degree, but the stocks of companies in the same industry – hotels, for example – tend to be fairly highly correlated, no doubt because their returns are driven by the same economic forces. This is why an investor seeking diversification of risk often sees to it that his or her portfolio contains securities in a variety of unrelated industries. This also explains why so many investors put a portion of their investment capital in domestic stocks, another portion in foreign stocks, and still other portions in investments such as bonds and real estate. In this way, if some securities are losing ground in the market, others are gaining. At the same time, the fiduciary charged with safeguarding and managing a client's funds through a diversified portfolio would be remiss in loading up the portfolio with securities representing a narrow slice of the economy, concentrating, for example, on medical-technology issues or airline stocks.

As more and more different and relatively uncorrelated securities are combined in a portfolio, the unique risks associated with the individual securities contribute less and less to the portfolio's "total risk." In other words, the unsystematic portion of total risk gradually disappears with diversification. Exhibit 3-4 indicates how unsystematic risk is gradually reduced as diversification increases.

Exhibit 3-4. Reducing Risk Through Diversification

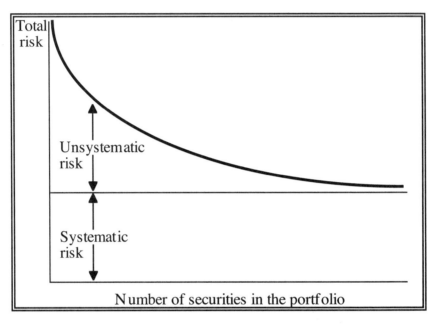

This allows us to present total risk in another form:

Total risk = Diversifiable risk + Nondiversifiable risk

With respect to common stocks, research indicates that given a systematic selection process, fifteen or twenty stocks grouped in a portfolio are sufficient to eliminate the unsystematic portion of total risk. Best of all, this lowering of total risk through diversification does not necessarily lower the investment's expected return – an important point to remember. To see how, consider Exhibit 3-5, which shows the return of two stocks, Alphatron and Betawhiz, both individually and when held in a portfolio. These stocks are perfectly negatively correlated with each other.

Exhibit 3-5A. Behavior of Alphatron

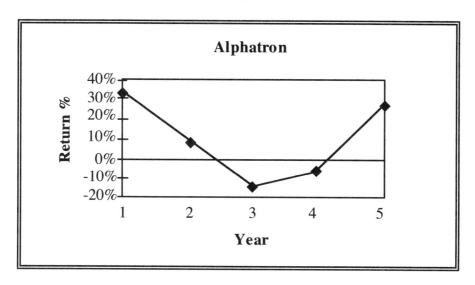

Exhibit 3-5B. Behavior of Betawhiz

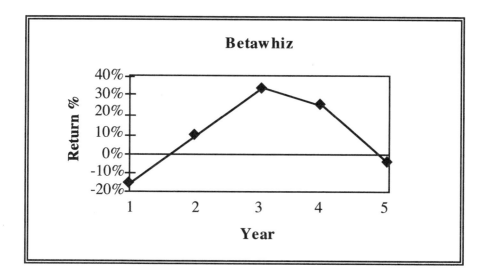

Exhibit 3-5C. Behavior of Alphatron and Betawhiz
          Combined

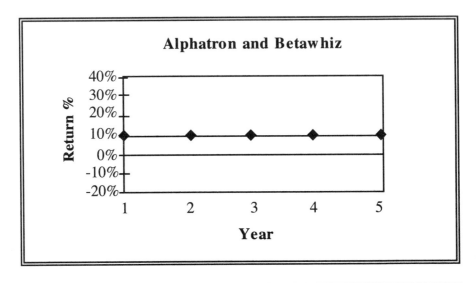

	Alphatron	Betawhiz	Portfolio
Year 1	35%	-15%	10%
Year 2	10%	10%	10%
Year 3	-15%	35%	10%
Year 4	-5%	25%	10%
Year 5	25%	-5%	10%
Avg. Rate of Return	10%	10%	10%
Standard Deviation	30%	30%	0%

The exhibit and accompanying data illustrate that while each stock has an average rate of return of 10% over the five year time horizon, and a standard deviation of 30%, the combined portfolio has the same rate of return, 10%, but 0% standard deviation. If the stocks in the portfolio were closely correlated, the returns would not have been smoothed out, and the standard deviation would not have been reduced significantly.

This ability to get the same expected return with less risk is the great benefit of diversification. As you already know intuitively, greater expected returns tend to go hand in hand with taking greater investment risks. So the ability to keep the level of return the same while lowering risk is a key benefit of diversification, and one of the things that investors typically expect from professional money management.

THE RISK/RETURN RELATIONSHIP

"Nothing ventured, nothing gained." This commonplace piece of wisdom describes in a nutshell one of the understandings of the investment art, namely, that usually, in the long-run, the expected returns of low risk investments tend to be modest when compared to high risk ventures, and vice versa. This is why "junk bonds" pay higher interest rates than treasury securities backed by the U.S. government, and it is why small company stocks have much higher expected returns in the long run than do common stocks of the nation's blue chip corporations. The greater expected returns are a function of the greater risk (uncertainty) borne by the investors.

The evidence for this risk/return relationship is both abundant and statistically solid. Exhibit 3-6 indicates the risk/return relationship for each major category of securities over a period of 69 years, as compiled by Ibbotson & Associates. As indicated, the highest returns and highest risk (as measured by standard deviation) are found in small company stocks. While many small firms go out of business, some will grow into the next Microsoft, Intel, and

MCI. Note also how the standard deviations change between the highest and lowest annual returns. The class of securities with the highest standard deviation, small company stocks, exhibits a tremendous range of returns.

Common stocks in general have provided a lower rate of return than small company stocks, but with less risk. And various categories of fixed income securities follow the same risk/return pattern.

This relationship between the risk and expected return of different classes of securities allows us to formulate what financial experts call the Capital Asset Pricing Model (CAPM). When this model is presented graphically, the straight line is referred to as the security market line (Exhibit 3-7). As the line indicates, high expected returns are associated with higher risk. In the exhibit, the relative position of different classes of securities are presented.

Exhibit 3-6. Returns and Standard Deviations for Major Classes of Securities

Classes of Securities	Annual Geometric Mean Return	Highest Annual Return	Lowest Annual Return	Standard Deviation
T-bills	3.7%	14.71%	-0.02%	3.3%
Long-term government bonds	4.8	40.36	-9.18	8.8
Long-term* corporate bonds	5.4	42.56	-8.09	8.4
Common stocks	10.2	53.99	-43.34	20.3
Small company stocks	12.2	142.87	-58.01	34.6

Source: © *Stocks, Bonds, Bills, and Inflation 1995 Yearbook*™, Ibbotson Associates, Chicago, (annually updates work by Roger G. Ibbotson and Rex A. Sinquefield). Used with permission. All rights reserved.

Exhibit 3-7. The Security Market Line

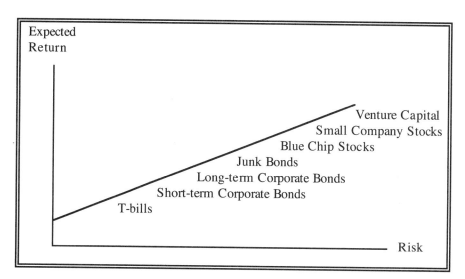

HOW WE MEASURE RETURN

Given this discussion of risk and return, it is fair to ask just how we go about measuring the return of a security or other investment. Return is the total gain to the investor over a given period of time. It includes dividends or other cash distributions received plus any capital appreciation (or less any capital losses). The rate of return during a fixed period of time is commonly calculated as follows:

$$\text{Rate of return} = \frac{(\text{ending value} - \text{beginning value}) + \text{cash dividends}}{\text{beginning value}}$$

Expressed another way:

$$\text{Rate of return} = \frac{\text{capital appreciation (or losses)} + \text{cash distributions}}{\text{inital price}}$$

For example, if a stock's price at the beginning of the year is $40, and that price rises to $46 at year-end, and if the stock pays out a $4 cash dividend, the return is equal to:

$$\text{Return} = \frac{(46-40)+4}{40} = 25\%$$

This is for one period. Another issue is measuring the rate of return for over a number of periods. In these cases, we rely on a more sophisticated technique. We continue to calculate the single period return as just described, but we express multi-period returns as either arithmetic or geometric average returns.

Consider a portfolio with the following characteristics:

	Time		
	Year 0	Year 1	Year 2
Value ($)	$100	$200	$100
Annual Rate of Return (%)	-	100%	-50%

The *arithmetic average* of the portfolio's rate of return is $\frac{(+100\%) + (-50\%)}{2} = 25\%$. Using the arithmetic average return suggests that an investor earned a 25% return over the two-year period. However, it is evident that the investor had a zero return over the two-year period. To confirm the zero return, we see that the average return over two years (R) is equivalent to the one year return reinvested for an additional year:

$$100(1 + R)(1 + R) = 100$$
$$100(1 + R)^2 = 100$$
$$R = 0\%$$

The zero return reflects what we call the *geometric average* return. Obviously, it better reflects the historical actual returns generated than does the arithmetic average. Interestingly, while the geometric return best describes historical returns, the arithmetic average best describes likely future performance. In other words, consider two equally likely outcomes, a gain of 100% ($100) and a loss of 50% (-$50). The expected profit on a $100 investment is $\frac{(\$100) + (-\$50)}{2}$ = $25, or 25%. The $100 profit in a good year outweighs the $50 loss in a poor year. Thus, the arithmetic return is often used as a guide to future investment returns.

In any case, the formulas for both arithmetic and geometric average returns are, of course, based upon actual market outcomes – actual capital appreciation and cash dividends that have been paid. Most investment decisions, however, concern the future, and so we use the term "expected" returns. "Expected" has another meaning that you should understand. The security market line in Exhibit 3-8 identifies the expected returns of various classes of investments, from risk-free T-bills to high risk venture capital. The expected returns fall neatly on the security market line. However, this is not to suggest that if an investor purchases the stock of a small company, for example, a high rate of return is preordained. It merely indicates that *on average* this class of stocks is expected to produce higher returns. Some have doubled and tripled their investors' money; others have resulted in total losses. On average, as measured over a relatively long period, small stocks have produced compound returns of over 12% per year.

Given what we noted earlier about the standard deviations for different types of investments, we can redraw our earlier security market line to show how actual returns may fall into a "range" that widens with the riskiness of the investment (see Exhibit 3-8). For a small stock investment with a given beta, for example, the "expected" return lies on the security market line itself, but the actual return might fall anywhere on the bold vertical line.

What you should take away from this exhibit is the understanding that the range of possible outcomes broadens as the investments chosen are riskier. For the low-risk investment, the range is very narrow, but for the high-risk investment the range includes major gains and major losses. Diversification makes it possible to come closer to the "expected" return.

Exhibit 3-8.   The Security Market Line With a Range of Possible Returns.

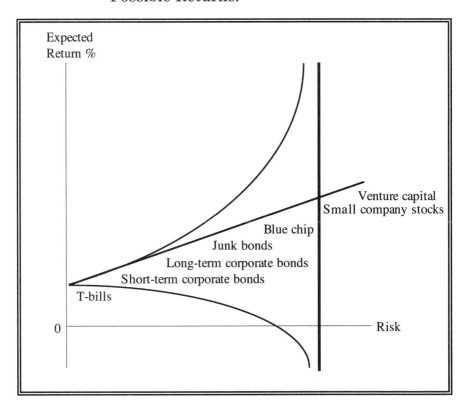

THE SCIENCE OF RISK AND RETURN: THE CAPM

Financial scholarship has provided a method for mathematically relating a security's non-diversifiable (systematic) risk to its expected return – what we have mapped in a general way on the security market line. This is the Capital Asset Pricing Model (CAPM). An application of this model is for calculating the risk-adjusted expected return for an individual stock or a portfolio.

Some of the terms in the CAPM should already be familiar. Beta, described earlier, is used as the measure of a security's non-diversifiable risk. The expected return is the combined return the investor expects to receive from cash dividends and capital appreciation. We will explain new terms as we move along. But first, here is the linear equation that represents the CAPM:

$$\text{The Expected Return} = R_f + \beta \times (R_m - R_f)$$

Where:

- R_f is the risk-free rate
- β is the beta (systematic risk) of the security or portfolio in question
- R_m is the market return
- $(R_m - R_f)$ is the "market premium" – the extra rate of return investors in a market portfolio expect to obtain above riskless investments (historically, in the 7%-9% range)

This equation can be rewritten as:

$$\text{The Expected Return} = R_f + \beta \times (\text{the market premium})$$

To see how this model could help us to estimate the expected return on common stock, consider this example:

Alphabyte stock has a beta (ß) of 1.20. The risk-free rate (R_f) – what investors currently receive from so-called riskless investments, such as 90-day T-bills – is 5%. If we use 7% as the market premium, an investor in Alphabyte will expect to earn the risk-free rate plus the market premium adjusted for the level of risk in this particular stock – its beta. Or, 5% +1.20 x 7% = 13.4%.

This example of the CAPM should confirm our understanding of the security market line described above. As illustrated in Exhibit 3-9, the line intersects the return axis at 5%, the risk-free rate. The expected return of Alphabyte stock is the sum of the risk-free rate, and the risk-adjusted market premium.

In this example, we have used a single stock, Alphabyte, and its beta to obtain an estimate of the expected return. Money managers extend this concept to entire portfolios, using the beta of the portfolio to estimate the portfolio's expected return.

While the CAPM is an ex-ante model, its parameters are typically determined historically. In other words, while the model is predictive, the beta and the market premium are obtained by considering past data. Also, there is an ongoing discussion among analysts whether the short-term treasury bill rate or the longer term treasury bond rate is the most appropriate risk-free rate. While the treasury bond may be more reflective of the holding period

Exhibit 3-9. Graphical Presentation of the CAPM

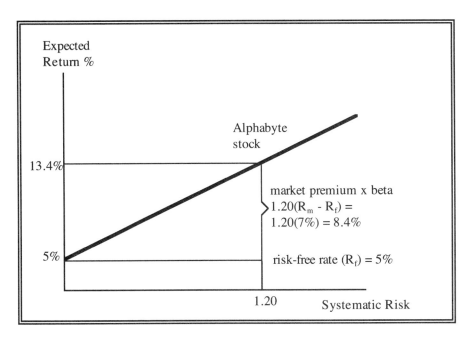

of the security, the treasury bill is the truly risk-free instrument.

EVALUATING INVESTMENT PERFORMANCE

By now, it should be clear that the expected return of a
well-diversified portfolio of securities should be a function
of its systematic risk – i.e., the risk that cannot be eliminated through diversification. Unfortunately, many inexperienced investors fail to recognize the relationship between risk and expected returns, and are mesmerized by
money managers who tout past returns of 20%-30%. Too
often, investors fail to ask the important question: "What
risks were taken in earning those high returns?" When we
evaluate investment performance of pension funds, mutual
funds, and other managed accounts we usually do not sim-

ply compare actual returns, but compare "risk-adjusted" returns. Fortunately, several practical approaches are available for doing that. In addition, it is often useful in a litigation context to be familiar with the relationship between an individual security's beta and a portfolio's beta.

Now we are ready for the discussion of risk-adjusted performance.

The Jensen measure. What is needed to evaluate investment performance is some measure that fully recognizes the amount of investment risk. Financial economist Michael Jensen developed such a measurement, one that fits nicely with the capital asset pricing model. The Jensen measure is the amount by which the actual returns of a portfolio exceed the return predicted by the CAPM. To appreciate his method, let's return to the concept of the security market line presented in Exhibit 3-10 with four investment portfolios: A, B, C and D. Both A and B, located on the security market line, have delivered returns that are appropriate given their respective risks. Portfolio A had a lower return than B, but also had lower systematic risk. Portfolio B produced a higher return than A, but subjected its investors to more risk. Thus, the investment managers for A and B, both performing along the security market line, did equally well.

Portfolio C is another story. This portfolio produced a return higher than its risk would justify. Given its level of risk, it produced a higher return than what we would have expected. The difference between the expected return and the actual return is commonly referred to as the portfolio's "alpha."

Either by skill or by luck, the money manager for C produced superior performance – a positive alpha. Normally, investors would have had to take on greater risk to

WHAT IS A PORTFOLIO BETA?

Earlier, we described the beta for individual securities. Portfolios are typically comprised of many securities – each with a different beta. Collectively, they form the portfolio beta. To calculate the portfolio beta, we must know the beta of each security as well as the percentage of total portfolio value it represents. We can then find the "weighted value" of these betas. Consider the three-stock portfolio below. Each stock has a different beta and each represents a different percentage of the total portfolio value.

Security	% of Total Portfolio Value	Beta
Stock A	20%	1.0
Stock B	30%	1.2
Stock C	50%	1.4

The weighted average beta, or the portfolio beta, is calculated by multiplying each stock's beta by its percentage of the value of the portfolio. This indicates the proportionate contribution of each stock to the overall portfolio beta. By summing these contributions, we obtain the portfolio beta. In this case:

Portfolio beta = (.20 x 1.0) + (.30 x 1.2) + (.50 x 1.4)
= 1.26

obtain these results. This is just the opposite from the case of Portfolio D, whose manager took the same level of systematic risk as B and C, but failed to achieve the "expected" rate of return. This portfolio had inferior performance – as measured by its negative alpha – delivering approximately the same return as low-risk portfolio A.

The position of a portfolio above or below the security market line determines its risk-adjusted performance according to the Jensen model.

Exhibit 3-10. The Performance of Four Portfolios

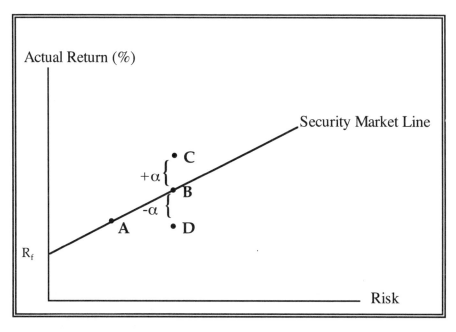

The Treynor performance index. Another method for measuring risk-adjusted return is the Treynor index. It divides the risk premium – the actual return that is above the risk-free return – by the level of risk, as determined by the beta of the portfolio. The Treynor index is derived as follows:

$$T_i = \frac{\text{total portfolio return - risk free rate}}{\text{portfolio beta}}$$

or

$$T_i = \frac{\text{risk premium}}{\text{portfolio beta}}$$

Given that the portfolio beta is a measure of its systematic risk, the Treynor performance index actually measures the risk premium (above the risk-free rate) per unit of systematic risk. Thus, if the manager of Fund A achieved a total return of 14% at a time when the risk-free rate was 5%, and the beta of the portfolio was 1.2, Fund A's Treynor index would be:

$$T_A = \frac{.14 - .05}{1.2} = 0.075$$

For the same time period, the manager of Fund B achieved a higher total return, 16%, holding a portfolio with a beta of 1.6. This fund's Treynor index would be:

$$T_B = \frac{.16 - .05}{1.6} = 0.069$$

The lower index of Fund B indicates that even though Fund B's total return was higher than A's, when accounting for its higher beta, its risk-adjusted performance was inferior to that of Fund A.

The Sharpe performance index. Like the Treynor index, the index developed by Nobelist William Sharpe divides the risk premium of a portfolio by a measure of its risk; but instead of using portfolio beta, the Sharpe index uses the portfolio's standard deviation. The formula for the Sharpe index is:

$$S_i = \frac{\text{total portfolio return - risk free rate}}{\text{portfolio standard deviation}}$$

or

$$S_i = \frac{\text{risk premium}}{\text{portfolio standard deviation}}$$

Given that the portfolio's standard deviation is a measure of the portfolio's total risk, Sharpe's performance index actually measures the risk premium (above the risk-free rate) per unit of total risk. For example, if Fund A's total return was 15% when the risk-free return was 5%, and the standard deviation of the portfolio was 10%, Fund A's Sharpe index would be:

$$S_A = \frac{.15 - .05}{.10} = 1.0$$

If Fund B, on the other hand, earned a total return of 10% during the same period but its portfolio standard deviation was 2.5%, the Sharpe index for Portfolio B would be:

$$S_B = \frac{.10 - .05}{.025} = 2.0$$

Therefore, although Fund A earned a higher total return, Fund B had a better risk-adjusted return based on the Sharpe performance index.

Benchmarking performance. The risk-adjusted methods of performance evaluation just described are precise and mathematical. However, we can obtain a general sense of investment performance by benchmarking the return on a particular portfolio against one of the many security indices. For example, if an investor owned a diversified portfolio of large, U.S.-based company stocks, its return could be compared to that of the Standard & Poor's 500 or the New York Stock Exchange Composite. Both serve as proxies for returns on stocks of this type. Likewise, if the investor's portfolio was comprised of small company stocks, the Russell 2000, an index based on 2000 small company stocks, would be an appropriate benchmark. The key, in any case, is to use the appropriate index, an identical time period, and to remember that the relevant performance indicated by the index should be based on all income such as dividends or interest being reinvested.

Exhibit 3-11 lists a number of publicly obtainable indices for stocks and fixed-income securities.

DEBT SECURITIES

Most of our discussion so far has involved the financial and investment characteristics of common stock. Debt securities constitute another, and much larger, category of securities. Debt securities are IOUs, and they are issued by governments, government agencies, and corporations.

Debt instruments come in dozens of forms. Most pay a fixed rate of interest on a regular basis. Some, such as U.S. Treasury bills and zero-coupon bonds, pay no interest at all, but are sold at a discount to face value which is paid at maturity. Others, such as mortgage-backed securities, pay security-holders a monthly distribution representing both interest and a return of their own capital. Still others, such as convertible bonds, can be "converted" from an interest-paying security into a predetermined number of common shares of the issuing company.

The variety and complexity of the debt security world cannot be adequately addressed in this section. Our intent here is mainly to describe the characteristics of the standard form of one type of debt security – the fixed rate bond – explaining the sources of its value, and providing a method for ascertaining its value. Litigation involving debt securities often involves the determination of value. Other cases involve requirements that issuers must meet with respect to bondholders.

Exhibit 3-11. Security Indices

Index	Contents	Comment
Dow Jones Industrial Average	30 actively traded blue-chip U.S. stocks	A narrow index of stock market activity. A major shift in a single security can move the index substantially
Standard & Poor's 500	500 widely-held U.S. common stocks: 400 industrials, 60 transportation and utilities, and 40 financial companies	Value-weighted – i.e., stocks with the greatest market capitalization have the greatest impact on the index
NYSE Composite	All stocks listed on the New York Stock Exchange (approx. 1,700)	A very broad-based, value-weighted index
Wilshire 5000	All NYSE, AMEX, and most active over-the-counter stocks	The broadest based index of U.S. common stocks
NASDAQ-OTC	Roughly 3,500 over-the-counter stocks	Weighted toward medium to smaller companies
Russell 2000	2,000 small companies	Reflects the greater volatility of small company stocks
Merrill Lynch Taxable Bond Index	Tracks 5,000 corporate and U.S. government bond issues	A broad measure of fixed income securities movements
Merrill Lynch International Bond Index	Major Eurobonds and foreign bonds	A measure of returns on non-U.S. debt securities

The standard corporate bond. The standard bond issued by U.S. corporations has these common features:

Face value. Sometimes call the "par value." This is the value of the bond at maturity. In most cases, it is the price at which the bond is originally issued.

Coupon rate. The stated annual interest rate payable to the bondholder.

Maturity date. The future date on which the issuer will redeem the bond at its par value.

Bond indenture. A legal statement spelling out the contractual obligations of the bond issuer and the rights of the bondholder.

Example. IBM issues new bonds to the public at a price of $1,000 each. The bonds have a par value of $1,000 payable at maturity on January 15, 2011. They pay an annual coupon of $90 (9% of $1,000), payable semi-annually. An indenture describes the details of how and when the bonds will be retired, where the bondholders stand relative to other holders of the company's debt, restrictions on the issuer's taking on more debt, and other details. The indenture is provided to a trustee charged with protecting the interests of bondholders.

Risks for bondholders. Although bonds, unlike stocks, contain explicit contractual obligations, bondholders are subject to a number of risks, some specific to the issuer, and others originating in the larger economic environment. These risks include the following:

- *Default risk.* Although a bond is a contractual obligation, an issuer that suffers a severe business reversal may not be able to pay interest and redeem the bonds at maturity. A compelling example of default risk was seen in the multi-billion dollar default of the well-publicized Washington Public Power Supply System.

- *Purchasing power risk.* Inflation undercuts the purchasing power of the investor's interest payments and redemption value.

- *Exchange rate risk.* A growing number of investors are purchasing bonds denominated in foreign currencies. These investors are exposed to the risk that the value of those currencies will decline against the U.S. dollar.

- *Liquidity risk.* The market for corporate bonds is generally less liquid than the market for the shares of those same companies. Bonds issued by smaller entities – sanitary districts, small municipalities, and so forth – are even less liquid. For bondholders this means that there may not be an active market should they want to sell their bonds.

- *Call risk.* Many bonds have a provision that permits the issuer to "call," or redeem the bonds prior to their stated maturity dates. Issuers love this provision because it gives them an opportunity to refinance their debts at lower rates when interest rates drop. Refinancing is bad news to investors, who run the risk of losing high-coupon bonds when rates begin to decline. Therefore, all other things being equal, a callable bond should promise a higher yield than a noncallable bond. (Some bonds offer "call protection" for a stated number of years subsequent to their issuance.)

• *Interest rate risk.* Rising interest rates generally reduce the market value of bonds held by investors.

The last characteristic merits special explanation.

We learned earlier that investors expect a certain
rate of return from a security, that rate being a function of
the security's risk. That expected return can fluctuate over
time. Suppose, for example, that investors require a 9%
return from a 15-year bond issued by a corporation with
IBM's level of risk. If, however, the general level of interest
rates were to rise, investors might require a 10% return
from these same bonds and others like them. The reverse
would be the case if the general level of rates declines.

The investor who holds the "IBM 9% of 2011" bonds
might sleep through changes in the interest rate environment. His interest checks would show up every six months
in the same amounts.   But if he kept in daily touch with
trading in the bond market, he'd have surely noticed that
the market value of his bonds rose when interest rates fell,
and fell when interest rates rose. This inverse relationship
is important to remember. The fixed coupon rate of 9%
acts as a fulcrum for the value of his bonds, as shown in
Exhibit 3-12. The coupon payment stays the same, but the
bond's market value moves in the opposite direction to
market interest rates.

The reason for this inverse relationship is easy to explain.
If investors can get 11% return from bonds with the same
default risk and the same number of years to maturity,
they will not pay $1,000 for the "IBM 9% of 2011." Intui-
tively, we know that they will pay less than $1,000. Just
how much less is determined through a calculation we will
describe later.

Exhibit 3-12. The Relationship Between the Market Value of Bonds and Interest Rates

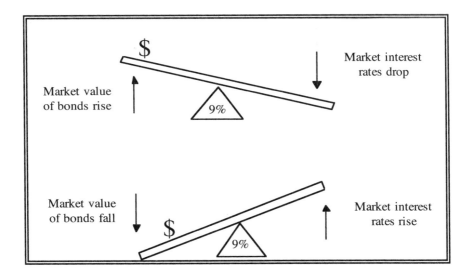

Yield-to-maturity.   Yield-to-maturity is the rate of return an investor will receive from a bond given its purchase price, stated interest rate (coupon rate), its value at maturity, and the time remaining to maturity.

Example. A General Motors bond purchased at its face value of $1,000, with a 10% coupon rate, and 5 years until maturity, has a yield-to-maturity (YTM) of 10%. Bonds trading in the secondary market, however, are rarely purchased at face value. For example, in an environment of higher interest rates, the GM bond just described may be trading at $900. It will continuing paying its stated interest payments of $100 (10% x $1,000), and will be redeemed at $1,000 upon maturity in 5 years. The YTM is the result of a time value calculation that recognizes these cash flows:

Year 0	Year 1	Year 2	Year 3	Year 4	Year 5
($900)	$100	$100	$100	$100	$100 $1000

The time value challenge here is to find a discount rate that will equate the present value of the cash flows in years 1 through 5 to the purchase price of $900. *This discount rate is the yield-to-maturity.* Financial calculators make this complex calculation simple. A discussion of yield-to-maturity can be found in the cost of capital chapter.

Bond valuation. A great many legal disputes involving debt securities revolve around the question: "What is the value of these bonds," or, in other cases, "What was their true value when they were sold to the bondholders?" As we will see in the chapter on bankruptcy and fraudulent conveyance, there have been cases in which the issuer or underwriter knowingly overstated the creditworthiness of the issuer, making it possible for the bonds to be issued at a lower interest rate than their riskiness would require. In determining the damages to bondholders in such cases, we need to do a valuation of the bonds in the absence of the fraud. To make this determination, we need a method for bond valuation.

Fortunately, the discounted cash flow method we have used so many times before is a powerful tool in determining the value of a bond. For example, if we were to calculate the yield-to-maturity (or discount rate) of the 5-year GM bond, we would know the price of the bond ($900), the size of each annual interest payment ($100), and the redemption value of the bond ($1,000) due at maturity in five years. We would find the discount rate that would re-duce the interest and principal repayment cash flows to $900.

In determining the value of a bond, we use the same method but have a slightly different set of knowns and un-knowns. In the case of the GM bond, we know that its re-demption value is $1,000, to be received at the end of the fifth year. And we know that each coupon payment will be $100 received at the end of years 1 through 5. Once we es-timate the return investors should receive from this par-ticular bond – given prevailing interest rates, the riskiness of the bond, and its five year term – we can calculate its value.

Let's say that market interest rates have just dropped, and that we determine that this bond should pro-vide a return (or YTM) of 9%. With 9% as our discount rate, we either use a table for the present value of a dollar or a financial calculator to discount the bond's future cash flows as illustrated in Exhibit 3-13.

Notice that the value of the bond is $1,039 – higher than its redemption value. This is not unusual when pre-vailing interest rates drop. Just remember that the value of a bond moves in the opposite direction of interest rate moves.

This valuation model should help you see the sources of bond value: the stream of coupon payments and the redemption value. These value sources are discounted by the required return, which is a function of the risk asso-ciated with the individual bond and with the overall eco-nomic and interest rate environment. Litigation involving debt securities will typically require an understanding of these relationships.

Exhibit 3-13. Determining the Value of a Bond

Present Value	Year 1	Year 2	Year 3	Year 4	Year 5	
	100	100	100	100	100	
92					1,000	redemption value
84					1,100	
77						
71						
715						
$1,039						

RISK MANAGEMENT AND DERIVATIVES

They are not securities, but contracts between two parties. For some investors they are tools for reducing market risk while for others they are tools for aggressive speculation. What are they? They are derivatives, a name that stems from the fact that their monetary value is "derived" from some other financial instrument: German marks, interest rates, a stock or stock index, and so forth. Generally designed and used as devices to manage financial risk, a number of companies have used them (perhaps unintentionally) to generate speculative profits. They have been a source of much litigation, largely stemming from gigantic losses. Gibson Greetings lost close to $20 million on a handful of complex derivatives that it claimed not to understand. That same month, Procter & Gamble took a $157 million derivatives loss. Orange County, California went bankrupt after it was hit with major losses. Guessing that interest rates were heading down, the county's investment officer used highly leveraged derivatives to back his gamble. But rates headed up, creating close to $1 billion in losses for the county's investment fund.

A highly publicized deal was the failure of the 230-year-old Barings Bank of London, bankrupted by a single, 27 year-old employee stationed in the Far East who used derivatives to bet on the direction of the Nikkei Stock Average index, Japan's equivalent of the Dow Jones Industrials.

Most derivatives are products of the age of financial innovation that began on Wall Street in the 1970s: options on listed stocks, interest rate futures, stock index futures and options, currency futures, and others. Over time, these derivatives became the building blocks for exotic strategies designed to either hedge financial risks or to engage in pure speculation. The terms interest rate swap, naked put, Libor-linked payout, and knock-out call option entered the lexicon of high finance.

An explanation of one basic derivative instrument in particular – the option – will help you appreciate this area of finance.

An option is a contract that gives its owner the right to either buy or sell a set quantity of a particular stock at a specified price within a specified period of time.

There are call options and put options. A call option gives the owner the right to buy, while a put option gives the owner the right to sell. For example, an AT&T 50 October call option gives its owner the right to "call," or buy, 100 shares of AT&T common stock at $50 per share any time before the option expires in October – no matter what the market price of AT&T stock may be. The owner of an AT&T 50 October put option has the right to "put" or sell, 100 shares of this stock at $50 per share at any time prior to the expiration date of the option. The price specified by the option is known as the strike price (also called the exercise price).

Naturally, there is a price to be paid for the right conferred by any option. There is no free lunch! This price is called the premium. For so-called "listed" options, those that trade daily on regular exchanges, the premium fluctuates daily as a function of five things:

- *Exercise or strike price.* The fixed price specified in the option contract at which the option buyer can purchase or sell the underlying asset. In the previous example, the exercise price was $50.
- *Time to expiration date.* The time remaining until the last date at which the option can be exercised.
- *Price of the underlying asset.* The price of the asset from which the option price is derived. In the example above, it is the price of AT&T common stock.
- *Volatility.* The standard deviation of the underlying asset returns.
- *Interest rate.* The risk free rate of an asset with the same maturity as the option.

The determinants of option value. It is early June, and you notice two quotations in the stock pages of the morning paper. One is for AT&T common stock, which closed yesterday at $53 per share; the other is for an AT&T 50 October call option. Its closing price yesterday was $6, or $600 for the right to purchase 100 shares of AT&T anytime between today and the expiration date at a price of $50 per share.

This option contract is said to be "in the money," since the share price is already higher than the exercise price of the option. The contract has an intrinsic value of $3 ($53 - $50). Intrinsic value is the amount by which the market price of the underlying stock is higher than the exercise price.

But why is the current value of this contract $6? What does the other $3 represent? The answer is that this contract has a time premium of $3. The time premium represents the opportunity for the stock to go still higher. In other words, it is the premium paid for the upside potential. Exhibit 3-14 separates the option premium of $6 into its two components: time premium and intrinsic value. If the price of AT&T held steady at $53 until the contract expiration in October, we would observe that the intrinsic value would stay the same, but the time premium would gradually evaporate as we draw closer to expiration.

The intrinsic value of a call option will fluctuate with the market price of the underlying stock; but the time premium will gradually diminish toward zero.

Before going any further, we should ask: "Why would anyone pay money for an option to buy or sell at a particular price?" To answer, let's consider three cases: one of a speculator, one of an option writer, and one of an investor who wants to hedge his risk.

The speculator. It is June, and Sheila Jones is aching to buy 100 shares of AT&T stock, which is currently trading at $53 per share. Sheila thinks this price is bound to go up sharply over the next several months, but most of her cash is tied up in other investments. Instead of buying the stock outright, she decides to buy one call option contract on AT&T. This contract has a strike price of $50, an October expiration, and is listed in the market at $6 (or $600 per 100-share contract). So, anytime before the option's expiration in October, Sheila can "call" 100 shares of AT&T at $50 per share – no matter what the market price is at the time.

Exhibit 3-14. Time to Expiration and Intrinsic Value

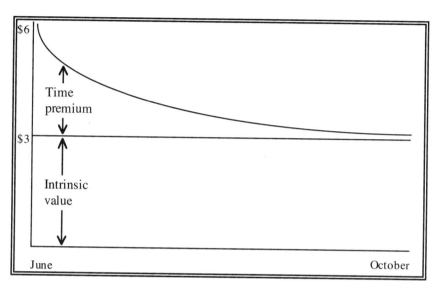

Sheila will break even on this transaction if AT&T stock rises to $56 – that would cover her option premium of $6 plus the cost of each share ($50). Anything above the $56 level will be profit for Sheila (not counting commissions). Exhibit 3-15 illustrates break-even and profits for Sheila at various AT&T stock prices.

Most speculators like Sheila never intend to exercise their options – i.e., "call" the stock on which their option is based. If they guess right about the direction of their stock's price, the price of the option itself will appreciate along with the underlying stock. Instead of calling the stock, they will simply sell the call option in the market, and take their profits from it. For example, if AT&T's stock price were to rise to $62 per share before October, Sheila's option value would rise to at least $12 (or $1,200).

She could simply sell her option and pocket at least a $600 profit (($12 - $6) x 100).

Exhibit 3-15. Break-Even and Profits (Losses) for a Call
            Option Buyer

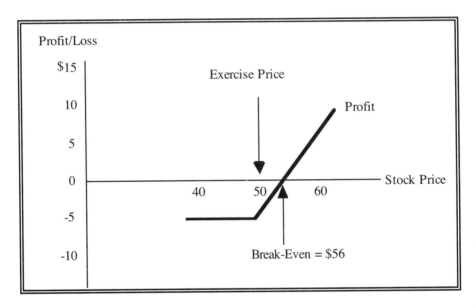

The Writer. For every optimist like Sheila, who is buying AT&T call options, there must be someone who sees the future differently, and who is selling options on the same stock. This person is often called the option writer. In this case, someone is willing to take Sheila's $600 premium in the belief that AT&T will not go up during the period of the option contract. This person is hoping that AT&T stock will languish through October, the option will expire unexercised, and he will have a $600 profit. There are two risks for this individual:

Note the leverage in the call-buying strategy. If things work out as described, and AT&T stock were to rise to $62, Sheila's $600 speculation would produce at least a $600 profit – a 100% return on her money in just a few months. Compare this to her return had she purchased the stock outright. In that case, she would have bought 100 AT&T shares for $5300 and sold for $6200 – a $900 profit on a $5300 investment, or a 17% return.

But leverage is a two-edged sword; if you can win big, you can also lose big. If the stock price failed to rise prior to expiration, Sheila would have lost 100% of her $600 venture.

1. If he already owns 100 shares of AT&T stock – making him a covered call writer – he will lose out on appreciation in the stock to the extent that it rises above $56 (the $50 strike price + the $6 premium) by October; or

2. If he does not already own 100 shares of AT&T stock – making him a naked call seller – his potential losses are theoretically unlimited. For example, if AT&T's stock shot up to $200 per share, he would be obliged to go into the market and purchase 100 shares at this price and sell them at $50 per share to someone like Sheila in order to satisfy his contractual obligation.

Exhibit 3-16 presents the break-even and profit situation for the covered call seller of an AT&T October 50 contract. The stock is currently trading at $53. As it indicates, the $6 premium earned through sale of the call option is kept as profit no matter how high the stock price goes. If

AT&T's market price drops, the call premium will offset losses by $6 per share, or down to $47 ($53-$6).

Exhibit 3-16. Break-Even and Profits (Losses) for a
              Covered Option Seller

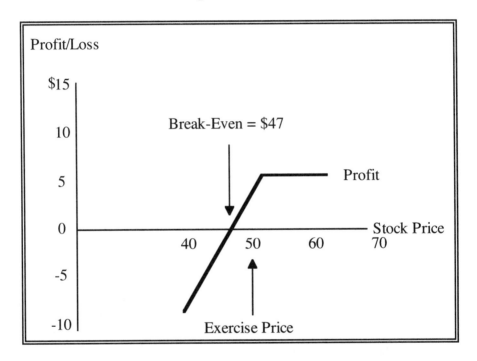

The hedger. Philip manages a multimillion dollar stock portfolio for a municipal employee pension fund. While the portfolio is broadly diversified, the stock market in general has been volatile, and Philip is fearful of a sharp market correction sometime soon.

Philip could avoid near-term losses by simply selling major portions of his stock portfolio and investing the proceeds in interest-paying securities, but that would result in large transaction costs. Faced with this situation, Philip decides to hedge his stock position by purchasing a number of stock index put options. If the value of his stocks drop, as feared, the value of the put options will increase, offsetting the losses. It is almost a form of insurance for which Philip will pay a premium.

Stock index options are based on one or another index. The Standard & Poor's 500 Index is typical. It is a mathematical representation of the share value of 500 widely-held U.S corporations. As such, it mirrors the collective rise and fall in the value of these stocks. Broadly diversified portfolios, such as Philip's – i.e., portfolios that contain 100-300 different stock issues representing many industries – move in close harmony with the S&P 500 index. This makes options on this index ideal as hedge instruments.

Derivatives for different purposes. While the option may be the simplest derivative to understand, you should know that a great many others exist. Other derivatives make use of *forward* and *future contracts*, which obligate a buyer and seller to exchange a certain quantity of an item at a specific price on a stated date. Futures contracts differ from forward contracts in that futures are traded on organized exchanges, while forwards are sold by financial institutions.

A *swap* is another popular form of derivative. Swaps are agreements to exchange future cash flows according to a pre-arranged formula. Many firms use them to hedge their exposure to interest rate fluctuations. In its simplest form, one party to the contract agrees to pay a fixed interest rate in return for receiving a floating rate from the other party.

The *convertible bond* is another, and more traditional form of derivative. This type of bond (or convertible preferred stock) contains a contractual provision that permits the bondholder to convert the bond (or preferred stock) into a certain number of the issuer's common shares.

Corporate treasurers are among the major financial hedgers. Multinational corporations deal in several major currencies whose market fluctuations can create turmoil on the bottom line of consolidated income statements. Such firms often enter into long-term purchase agreements and investments that expose them to major losses if interest rates or currency rates fluctuate greatly.

Example. A corporation agrees to purchase $20 million worth of German-built machine tools over the next two years. These purchases must be paid in German marks. The corporate treasurer could bet that the dollar-mark exchange rate will stay the same or that the dollar will gain or lose value against the mark over the next two years. But corporate treasurers are not in the wagering business. To assure a relatively predictable cost to the firm for these purchases, she enters into a currency futures contract on the mark.

Example. Boeing issues a 10-year convertible bond with an 8% interest rate at its face value of $1,000 per bond. The bond may be converted into 20 common shares of Boeing by the bondholder at any time during the life of the bond. Boeing shares are trading in the market at $42 at the time the bond is issued.

Convertibles have advantages for both issuers and investors. Issuers whose bonds have this convertibility feature can usually sell the bonds at a slightly lower interest rate than "straight" bonds. This reduces their interest expense. On the other hand, investors in convertibles receive interest payments and an opportunity for capital gains if the value of the common stock rises above a certain level. In the Boeing example above, that opportunity would be represented by any Boeing stock price above $50. For example, if Boeing stock rose to $55 per share, the holder of a $1,000 convertible bond could exchange it for 20 shares having a total market value of $1,100 (20 x $55).

Another common derivative is the *warrant*, which is an option issued by a corporation enabling the investor to purchase its common stock at a specified price (the strike price) within a specified period of time. These are generally issued in conjunction with the issuance of another security as a "sweetener" to induce their purchase by investors.

Example. General Film Corporation, whose shares are currently trading at $50, issues 250,000 new common shares in a public offering. Each of the new shares has an attached warrant which can be used to purchase an additional share at $70 per share at any time prior to January 31, 2016. After that date, the warrants expire.

Like the listed options described earlier, warrants may have an intrinsic value and a time premium. In the case of General Film warrants, above, there is no intrinsic value, as the exercise price is above the price of shares available in the market. With many years before their expiration, however, each warrant may have a significant time premium, which is determined by investors' expectations of the company's future. Warrants frequently begin trading in secondary markets shortly after their issuance.

Based on publicly available information, the Procter & Gamble case against Bankers Trust involved two highly complex swap agreements which P&G originally entered into with Bankers Trust. Under the terms of a typical swap, a company will exchange its fixed rate debt payments for floating-rate debt payments, or vice versa. The company that swaps into fixed rate payments is hedging against rising interest rates. P&G, however, swapped for floating rates, effectively betting on a drop in interest rates.

The original contract was for $200 million and had very unique terms. For the first six months of this agreement, P&G locked in a fixed rate interest payment of 0.75% below the commercial paper rate. After six months, the interest rate would float and would be linked to a complex formula based on the 5-year and 30-year treasury rates, among others. Had interest rates continued to slide or remain low, P&G would have saved up to $1.5 million per year (0.3% of its total annual interest expense) for a total potential savings of $7.5 million – pocket change for a company the size of P&G. If interest rates rose, as they did, the company would be exposed to significant losses.

The first six months of the deal saw the relevant treasury rates rise significantly. P&G responded by entering into yet another complex swap with Bankers Trust, speculating, once again, that rates would soon fall. This new agreement was called a "wedding band" because the company would realize savings if rates remained in a narrow range, or band. If rates rose or fell outside the band, however, the company's interest rate would be based on another complex formula involving a base rate plus ten times the difference between the swap rate and 4.5%. We warned you that these things could be confusing.

As interest rates rose, P&G came face-to-face with the magnitude of its losses. As it unraveled its derivative strategy with Bankers Trust, it came out of the affair with a reported loss of $157 million. It would have to sell lots of soap and disposable diapers to make up for the loss.

The question is whether Bankers Trust fully explained the potential for losses in the contracts it sold to P&G, and whether it correctly apprised its client of the profit/loss status of its derivative investment. Obviously, a potential counterargument is that P&G was a "sophisticated investor." In fact, P&G had bet successfully on falling interest rates in the past. But in the end, its involvement in this complex swap exposed it to tremendous losses. For its part, the company alleged that its management was misled by experts at Bankers Trust, and pursued a lawsuit against it based on these two swap agreements.

COMMON AREAS OF SECURITIES LITIGATION

When an individual or a pension fund loses a significant portion of its portfolio value, the money manager is sometimes accused of mismanaging the account's assets. Very often, the focus of litigation is around one of several issues: "churning" of the account, imprudent management, or some form of fraud.

Churning. "Churning" is the colloquial term used to describe excessive trading in an investor's account. Stockbrokers are compensated almost entirely in the form of commissions generated through their buying and selling activities. They may spend a great deal of time listening to clients and suggesting investment strategies, but they do not get paid until a commission-generating transaction takes place. Every time a client solicits a transaction or agrees to a broker's recommendation to buy or sell a security, the broker and his firm split the transaction commission. This compensation system places brokers in the ambiguous position of giving objective investment advice while having a financial interest in a high level of account activity.

While SEC rules prohibit account churning, it does happen, particularly when inexperienced investors fall into the hands of unscrupulous brokers. In technical terms, churning is often measured by the turnover ratio of the portfolio. Whether the account is invested in a variety of securities (e.g., stocks, bonds, governments) or in only one type of security, portfolio turnover is often determined by considering all securities held. It is calculated by determining the lesser of the total amount of securities bought or sold in a given time period divided by the average market value of the portfolio. In its simplest form, the average market value is calculated by adding the beginning portfolio market value to the ending portfolio market value and dividing the result by two. Exhibit 3-17 provides the information needed for the turnover ratio calculation.

Exhibit 3-17. Information Needed for the Turnover Ratio
                          Calculation

	Trading Activity	
	Purchases	Sales
Stock Holdings	$1,175,000	$1,150,000
Bond Holdings	1,100,000	875,000
Total	$2,275,000	$2,025,000
	Market Values	
	January 1	December 31
Stock Holdings	$700,000	$750,000
Bond Holdings	600,000	625,000
Total	$1,300,000	$1,375,000

First, we determine the lesser of the total amount of securities bought or sold. In this case, the lesser amount is $2,025,000. Next we find the average market value of the portfolio, which is:

$$\frac{\$1,300,000+\$1,375,000}{2} = \$1,337,500$$

The turnover ratio for this portfolio is:

$$\frac{\$2,025,000}{\$1,337,500} = 1.5$$

This turnover ratio itself carries little meaning. It is only when we compare it to turnover within other similar portfolios that implications about churning become clear.

Moreover, one has to consider the effect of any forced liquidations (from bonds being called, or stocks liquidated through mergers or buyouts) or the client's own request to liquidate part or all of the portfolio. In one case we encountered, the money managers were ordered to liquidate the entire portfolio within a short time period, creating an unusually high turnover ratio.

In litigation, the question "What is excessive turnover?" is not easily answered. What if the turnover ratio was five and investment performance was exceptional? Was the turnover ratio damaging to the client? At the other extreme, what can be said of a portfolio with poor performance and almost no turnover? Is the money manager liable for being too inactive in his trading activity?

Fortunately, the mutual fund industry provides an abundance of information on turnover rates and rates of return broken down by fund category. Morningstar, Wilshire Associates, and Nelson Publications are some of the principal sources.

Imprudent management. Severe losses in an investment portfolio are often at the heart of litigation, with the account owner claiming that the money manager was negligent in his or her management of the portfolio. For stock portfolios, the Jensen, Treynor, and Sharpe measures described earlier are useful gauges of the manager's risk-adjusted performance, especially when comparing the indices of the particular portfolio to a benchmark index. Other features of the portfolio to examine include the following:

- *Suitability.* Investment advisors, brokers, and money managers are obliged to determine the objectives of their clients, and their financial capacities to invest and assume risks. Investment strategies and security selection are expected to flow from this determination. If an investor had listed "preservation of capital" as a prime objective, a portfolio filled with high risk stocks would be a red flag in terms of "suitability." Standard deviations and betas are credible measures of risk and are available for many stocks; those that are not available can be calculated. Likewise, many bonds are rated by credit agencies (Duff & Phelps, Fitch Investors Service, Moody's and Standard & Poor's).
- *Diversification.* As explained earlier, the failure to diversify exposes the portfolio to added risk without increasing the expected return. Diversification can be gauged by 1) determining the number of securities in the portfolio, and 2) determining the extent to which those securities are correlated. In general, if the securities are selected from a broad range of industries, they will not be closely correlated and the benefits of diversification will most likely be realized. The number of different Standard Industrial

Classification (SIC) codes represented in the account can be used as a measure of this diversification across industries.

- *Investment strategy.* A key to determining a manager's prudence can often be found in a prospectus or brokerage agreement. These documents identify either the money manager's intentions or the investor's goals, and they can be used as yardsticks to measure the appropriateness of actual investments and transactions. Do the investments and transactions indicate adherence to stated strategy?

Failure to disclose. Public companies are required by law to disclose all relevant information. Litigation occurs when investors believe that full disclosure of material information has not been made, and also when they believe that misleading statements have been made. One form of disclosure litigation is fraud on the market.

Fraud on the market. In an interview with a major business weekly, the CEO of Stall Automotive Corporation recounts his firm's winning of a major contract to supply equipment to leading auto makers. "This should boost our earnings by $3.5 million during the next quarter and every quarter thereafter for several years," he crows.

Securities markets in the United States are sufficiently efficient that statements such as this one are picked up and quickly reflected in the price of a company's shares. If the information is new or unanticipated, it can move share prices considerably.

For illustration purposes, let's suppose that the CEO in this story was revealing new information, and that $3.5 million in added earnings represented a major earnings increase for his company. Chances are that Stall Automotive's shares would rise in the market, and a number of investors would purchase them at this higher price. Suppose further that the CEO's rosy projections were made fraudulently, perhaps to inflate the market value of the company shares at a time when he wanted to sell his own holdings. This potentially would be a case of fraud on the market. More formally, fraud on the market requires several conditions, including:

- public misrepresentation or failure to disclose material facts during the relevant period of time;
- material omission and misrepresentations;
- artificial maintainance or inflation of the company's security prices; and
- acquisition of securities by shareholders during the time in which the company failed to disclose or misrepresented material facts, and before the time the true facts were fully disclosed.

Typically, once the truth of the matter is publicly revealed, the actions of buyers and sellers drive down the price of those shares, create a loss for many who purchased shares subsequent to the fraudulent representation. The legal theory underlying fraud on the market holds that if a fraudulent statement or act results in the improper pricing of a security, those responsible for the statement or act may be liable to investors.

While the merits of liability in such cases may be straightforward, determining damages is very complex. One method is called market model damage analysis. In this analysis we attempt to determine the difference between the security's historical price inflated by the effect of fraud and what the security's price would have been absent the fraud. The first part of this chore is easy: we simply use public information to plot the daily trading prices of the security during the period of the fraud. In Exhibit 3-18, we use the hypothetical case of Stall Automotive, whose CEO made the fraudulent statement on July 1st. Public knowledge of the fraud was made known several weeks later, at which time the stock price dropped sharply.

Exhibit 3-18. Stall Automotive Stock Prices and its
Estimated True Value

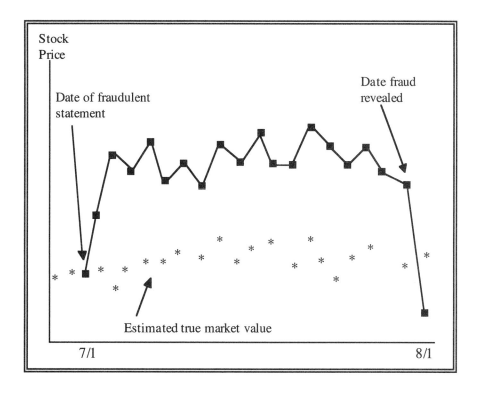

More difficult to figure is the value of the stock during this period in the absence of fraud – i.e., what Stall stock would have been had the fraud not been committed. To find this value on a daily basis, one can use the concept of beta, which tells us how much Stall would be "expected"

to move – and in which direction – relative to a move in the stock market in general. If Stall had a beta of 1.0, for example, a 1% rise in the market (the S&P 500 or other relevant index) on a given day would be expected to produce approximately a 1% rise in the price of Stall. Following this concept, one would obtain the change in the market index and multiply it by the beta of Stall to calculate each day's expected move. In Exhibit 3-18, these expected values are shown in the lower line of dots. The difference between the fraud induced share price and the estimated non-fraud market price on any given date can be used to determine damages to investors.

Chapter 4

The Cost of Capital

The cost of capital is one of the most important concepts used in business. To managers, it is the "hurdle rate" that any new investment in acquisitions, equipment, or projects must exceed to be worth doing. In the simplest terms, if a company's cost of capital is 15%, then any of its new business investments must have *at least* a 15% rate of return to be considered for funding.

Lawyers also have numerous uses for the cost of capital, which include the following:

- Purchase or sale of a business
- Merger or buyout
- Divestiture or acquisition of a division
- Warrant or option valuation
- Bankruptcy and reorganization
- Contract violation and resulting damages

In each of these situations one must assess value, whether it be for a company, division, or stream of cash flows. We've already seen how the discounting of future cash flows to their present value is a powerful tool in determining the value of a business. As part of the valuation process, one must ask: what is the appropriate discount rate? The answer: the company's cost of capital. This approach has powerful uses in each of the situations listed above. In bankruptcy cases, for example, creditors must often determine whether a company is of greater value as an ongoing business or as a set of saleable assets. As a result, an important input to the decision process is the cost of capital.

In cases involving damages from contract violations, lost future sales result in the loss of future cash flows. We need to express those future losses as present values. And again, an appropriate discount rate is part of the solution. The appropriate rate is the company's cost of capital.

THE COST OF CAPITAL FOR A BUSINESS

The cost of capital for a business is the return (expressed as a percentage) that its creditors and shareholders expect to receive. Many people mistakenly think that cost of capital is simply the company's cost of borrowing money. As we'll soon see, the cost of borrowing is the relevant cost only for loans to the company and for other IOUs, such as bonds. But shareholders also have expectations for returns, and the cost of meeting their expectations is a component of the company's overall cost of capital.

As a prelude to any discussion of cost of capital, we need to consider a firm's sources of capital – i.e., how a firm is financed. Consider the example of SkyWarrior Software, a developer of computer games. Its simplified balance sheet, shown in Exhibit 4-1, indicates two sources of capital: debentures (unsecured bonds), and stockholders' equity. The debentures in this case are bonds that mature in 10 years. They pay their holders interest at a rate of 14%.

We can see from this balance sheet that the total long-term capital employed in the business (the debentures plus stockholders' equity) is $250 million. Obviously, some funds are also being provided through current liabilities. In all likelihood, these would include accounts payable, accrued taxes, accrued wages, and perhaps a bank loan of less than one year. (In the world of finance, "current" sources of funds – those due in less than one year – are usually not thought of as capital. Capital is typically a more permanent source of funding.)

Exhibit 4-1. SkyWarrior Software, Inc. Balance Sheet
   ($ millions)

Assets		Liabilities	
Current assets	$330	Current liabilities	$150
Net plant & equipment	70	Debentures	150
		Stockholders' equity	100
Total assets	$400	Total liabilities and equity	$400

The purpose of ascertaining SkyWarrior's capital structure is to understand what proportion is represented by long-term debt, and what proportion by equity. Here debt and equity are 60% and 40% respectively. Understanding this, we can begin to calculate the company's cost of capital, which is the "weighted average" of the cost of debt and the cost of equity capital, or WACOC.

For SkyWarrior Software, the weighted average cost of capital is represented by the following equation:

WACOC = .60 x (cost of debt) + .40 x (cost of equity)

THE COST OF DEBT

Determining the cost of debt is usually more straightforward than assessing the cost of equity. The cost of debt is the interest rate (or yield) that the firm must promise to creditors to induce them to provide long-term funds. In the case of SkyWarrior Software, which has a single source of debt, determining the cost of debt would appear simple. But most companies, especially larger ones, have many sources of debt with a complex set of features, issued at different interest rates. This complicates the job of calculating the cost of debt.

Consider the case of Macy's Department Stores, which after its leveraged buyout had the following debt on its balance sheet (Exhibit 4-2):

Exhibit 4-2. Macy's Cost of Debt

Type of Debt	Interest Rate (%)	Amount (millions)	Portion of Total Debt
Existing (pre-LBO) long-term debt	8.0	$120	0.04
Real estate mortgage	11.0	800	0.27
Bank loan	12.0	795	0.26
Senior notes	13.5	200	0.07
Senior subordinated debentures	14.5	400	0.13
Subordinated debentures	15.5	450	0.15
Subordinated discount debentures	17.0	250	0.08
Total		$3,015	1.00

As illustrated in the exhibit, the largest debt component is an $800 million real estate mortgage, and the smallest is $120 million in existing (pre-LBO) long-term debt. The exhibit provides the interest rate charged on each of these debt instruments and their respective weights as a percentage of Macy's total debt. To determine the cost of debt in this case, we multiply the interest rate by the weight of this type of debt as a percentage of total debt, and then sum as shown below:

Macy's cost of debt = (.04 x 8.0) + (.27 x 11.0) + (.26 x 12.0) + (.07 x 13.5) + (.13 x 14.5) + (.15 x 15.5) + (.08 x 17.0) = 12.93%

We use the example of post-LBO Macy's here for a particular reason: with the exception of the $120 million in existing (pre-LBO) debt, the debt on its balance sheet was assumed as part of the leveraged buyout. In contrast, the debt of the typical large corporation is acquired over some period of time. For example, on the books of a company we may find one set of debentures issued twenty years ago at 6%, and another set of debentures issued last week at 12%. Obviously, the cost of debt for this firm today is very far from 6%. And it is today's cost of debt that matters. Financial scholars call this the "marginal cost of debt" – i.e., the cost of acquiring the next block of debt capital.

Since debt on the books of a company is historical, and the cost of that debt is rarely a true indicator of the current cost of debt, what practical approach can we use to determine what a company's cost of debt is today?

For companies with publicly traded debt securities, the yield-to-maturity of their securities is a good rule-of-thumb. Yield-to-maturity indicates what rate of interest is needed to induce an investor to buy or hold a company's debt.

Recalling our discussion of bond valuation in our chapter on securities, yield-to-maturity (YTM) is the rate of return that an investor will receive from a bond given its purchase price, stated interest rate (coupon rate), its value at maturity, and the time remaining to maturity.

If a bond is purchased at its face value, the YTM is the same as the stated coupon rate. But bonds trading in the market are rarely purchased at face value. They are either bought at a discount to the face value or at a premium. For example, in an environment of lower interest rates, consider a bond that was issued at face value when interest rates were higher, say 8%, and is now trading at $1041. It will continue paying its stated interest payments of $80 (8% x $1,000), and upon maturity will be redeemed at $1,000. The YTM is the result of a time value calculation that recognizes these cash flows. For a 5-year bond with an 8% coupon assumed to be paid annually, and purchased at $1041, we'd have these cash flows:

Year 0	Year 1	Year 2	Year 3	Year 4	Year 5
($1041)	$80	$80	$80	$80	$ 80 $1000
					$1080

Yield-to-maturity is the discount rate that will equate the present value of these cash flows to the purchase price of $1041. Financial calculators make this calculation easy. Simply follow these steps:

$$PV = -1041, \ PMT = 80, \ n = 5, \ FV = 1000$$

Depending on the particular calculator, derive the YTM by computing or solving for "i," which in this case is 7%.

Adjustment for taxes. Since interest costs are tax-deductible, it stands to reason from the firm's perspective that the effective cost of debt must be figured on an after-tax basis.

You probably know how to make this calculation from your own experience with tax-deductible interest. For instance, if the interest rate on your mortgage is 9%, you can figure your after-tax interest rate as follows:

After-tax interest rate = 9% x (1-your tax rate).

If you are in the 40% tax bracket, this equates to 9% x (1-.40), or 5.4%. In other words, on an after-tax basis, your mortgage costs you 5.4%.

We adapt this approach in determining the after-tax cost of debt for a company. Here we use the formula:

$$\begin{pmatrix} \text{After tax} \\ \text{cost of debt} \end{pmatrix} = \begin{pmatrix} \text{Pre tax cost} \\ \text{of debt} \end{pmatrix} \times (1 - \text{tax rate})$$

Example. If we determine that Macy's pre-tax cost of debt is 12.93%, and its tax rate is 50%, its after-tax cost of debt is:

$$12.93 \times (1 - .50) = 6.47\%$$

THE COST OF EQUITY

While determining a company's cost of debt may well be a nontrivial task, ascertaining its cost of equity is even more complex. Fortunately, the capital asset pricing model (CAPM), which was explained in our chapter on securities, is an effective tool for determining the cost of equity.

CAPM revisited. The cost of equity for a firm is the lowest rate of return necessary to induce investors to buy or hold a firm's stock. This rate of return equals the risk-free rate plus a premium for risk. In other words, it has components representing a basic return on money and a return that compensates the investor for risk. This is exactly how we described the capital asset pricing model:

Cost of equity = R_f + (ß x the market premium)

where R_f is the risk-free rate, and ß is the beta of the particular stock – a measure of its volatility relative to the market as a whole. Recalling the securities chapter, the market premium is the difference between the risk-free rate and the long-term return on the market as a whole (R_m - R_f). This market premium is about 7%-9%.

Example. SkyWarrior has a beta of 1.5, meaning that its market price movements are 50% more volatile than the stock market as a whole (the beta of the market is 1.0). If the market premium is 7% and the risk-free rate is 5%, the cost of equity for SkyWarrior is:

Cost of equity = .05 + (1.50 x .07) = .155 or 15.5%

The dividend growth model. In some cases it is possible to estimate a company's cost of equity using another approach, the dividend growth model. This model equates the cost of equity with the sum of the stock's dividend yield and the expected growth rate of dividends. In other words:

$$\begin{pmatrix} \text{Cost} \\ \text{of equity} \end{pmatrix} = \begin{pmatrix} \text{Dividend} \\ \text{yield} \end{pmatrix} + \begin{pmatrix} \text{Expected} \\ \text{dividend} \\ \text{growth rate} \end{pmatrix}$$

or

Cost of equity = D/P + g

where:
D is the expected dividend for the coming year,
P is the current stock price, and
g is the expected dividend growth rate.

Example. SkyWarrior Software is paying an annual dividend of $2 per share, and its dividend has been growing at an annual rate of 11%. The current stock price is $40. We can estimate its cost of equity as:

Cost of equity = 2/40 + .11 = .16, or 16%.

This figure is very close to the 15.5% cost of equity determined through the CAPM.

The tricky part of using this model, of course, is obtaining a reliable number for g, the expected growth rate of the firm's dividends. We may look backward or forward to determine g. Looking backward, we can determine the historical growth rate of dividends and then possibly assume that future growth will follow the same pattern. In the long-run, however, future dividends are driven by future earnings, and not by history, and so any determination of g should recognize expectations of future earnings. For larger companies, estimated growth rates are generally available from Value Line or similar investment information services. For smaller companies, local and regional brokerage firms often provide research that estimates future earnings growth.

Many companies, of course, pay no dividends. For them, the traditional form of the dividend growth model is difficult to apply.

The bond yield plus risk premium approach. A third approach, but more of a "rule of thumb", to estimate the cost of equity is to simply add some amount, say 4%, to the interest rate of a company's long-term debt. The 4% in this case simply represents the added risk of being a common shareholder instead of a debt holder.

Example. We find that the pre-tax cost of long-term debt for SkyWarrior Software is 12%. Adding 4% to this gives us a cost of equity of 16%.

Cost of equity and taxes. In our earlier section on cost of debt, we noted that the cost of debt should be stated on an after-tax basis, since debt payments are generally tax-deductible for a business. No such adjustment is made in the case of cost of equity, since stock returns to shareholders (capital appreciation and dividends) are not tax-deductible for the firm.

The effect of financial leverage on the cost of equity. Financial leverage is often measured by the debt-to-equity ratio of a company's capital structure. The greater the ratio (the greater the percentage of debt), the greater the leverage. A company with no debt and $10 million of equity in its capital structure has a debt-to-equity ratio of zero ($0/$10) and no financial leverage. If the proportion is $2 million debt to $8 million equity, the ratio is 25% ($2/$8) and the company is using leverage.

Financial leverage magnifies the effects of profits and losses of a business. As a result, greater financial leverage is closely related to the volatility of returns, which can be measured by beta. Put another way, higher financial leverage is associated with a higher company beta.

The Macy's case provides a powerful example of the effects of financial leverage on the riskiness of returns and the cost of a company's equity. Again, because the giant retailer was rapidly transformed by a leveraged buyout from a state of low leverage to high leverage, we can observe the effects of leverage on the company's cost of equity.

THE IMPACT OF FINANCIAL LEVERAGE ON THE BOTTOM LINE

Financial leverage magnifies the returns to business own-ers. To understand this important principle of finance, consider the following example. Gravitz Corporation is capitalized by $5 million of stockholders' equity. There are no borrowed funds in its capital structure. Its earnings af-ter taxes are $1 million. Therefore, the stockholders re-ceive a 20% return on their capital investment ($1/$5).

Holden Corporation, on the other hand, operates with mostly borrowed money. Like Gravitz, it uses $5 mil-lion of capital, but $4 million is long-term debt and only $1 million represents the invested capital of stockholders – or equity. Holden's bottom-line earnings are $0.5 million – less than Gravitz's because it had to make interest pay-ments on its debt. But the returns to its shareholders are a whopping 50% ($0.5/$1).

The reason for the difference is financial leverage.

Leverage is, however, a two-edged sword. The effects of losses, like the effects of gains, are magnified by finan-cial leverage. Also, the contractual obligation to make in-terest payments on debt reduces earnings in good years, and can easily plunge a company into red ink during bad years. Together, these effects of financial leverage increase the downside risk to suppliers of equity capital.

To appreciate the risk of financial leverage, consider what would happen if both companies suffered a $1 million loss. Gravitz investors would experience a 20% loss on their $5 million equity stake. For Holden shareholders, on the other hand, the $1 million loss would entirely wipe out their $1 million investment.

Prior to the LBO, Macy's had a debt-to-equity ratio of 14.6% and a beta of 1.10. Using our knowledge of Macy's beta with leverage ($ß_L$), its tax rate and its debt-equity ratio, we can estimate Macy's beta (market risk) as if it had no debt. This "unlevered beta" ($ß_u$) is found as follows:

$$ß_L = ß_u \times [1 + (1 \text{ - tax rate}) \times \frac{\text{debt}}{\text{equity}}]$$

or

$$1.10 = ß_u \times [1 + (1 - .50) \times 0.146]$$
$$ß_u = 1.02.$$

This figure, 1.02, is often referred to as the unlevered beta, or operating beta. Using it and our original equation, we can find the new beta for the post-LBO Macy's, which became loaded with debt. But first, we must find its new debt-equity ratio. Given that the post-LBO Macy's had $3.015 billion debt and only $300 million in equity, the post-LBO debt-equity ratio was 10.05. Substituting these values into our equation, we find that

$$\text{Macy's Post-LBO Beta} = 1.02 \times [1 + (1 - .50) \; 10.05]$$
$$= 6.15$$

This is an amazingly high beta and a real exception in the world of corporate finance! But then its debt-equity ratio of 10.05 is equally high.

Now the payoff.

With this new beta, we can calculate the cost of equity for the post-LBO Macy's using our traditional CAPM formula of:

Cost of equity = risk-free rate + (ß x market premium)

or

Cost of equity = .05 + (6.15 x .07) = 0.48, or 48%

where the risk-free rate is 5% and the market premium is 7%. In other words, Macy's high debt increases its beta which in turn drives its cost of equity to 48%.

CALCULATING THE WEIGHTED AVERAGE COST OF CAPITAL

Over the course of this chapter, we've estimated Macy's post-LBO after-tax cost of debt as 6.47% and its cost of equity as 48%. The next, and final, step is to use these figures in determining the firm's weighted average cost of capital. Let's summarize what we know as follows:

Type of Capital	Cost (%)	Amount ($ millions)	Weight
Debt	6.47	3,015	0.91
Equity	48.00	300	0.09
Total		3,315	1.00

If Macy's capital structure was half debt and half equity, we could simply add 6.47% and 48% and divide the sum by two. In other words, a simple average. Recall, however, that the company's post-LBO capital structure is 91% debt and 9% equity. So we need to reflect these weights in determining the weighted average cost of capital as follows: -

WACOC = .91 x (cost of debt) + .09 x (cost of equity)

WACOC = (.91 x .0647) + (.09 x .48) = .102, or 10.2%

Thus, Macy's weighted average cost of capital is 10.2%. How does the attorney use a cost of capital once it is obtained? Consider the following examples:

Case A. You are a lawyer for Aaron's Furniture, and a team of its executives has shown you a plan for the acquisition of a regional retail store chain. The target's value could be determined by discounting its estimated future cash flows by its cost of capital.

Case B. As an attorney for Alex Software, you have successfully demonstrated in court that a rival company has infringed on an Alex copyright in creating its own version of one of Alex's most successful products. Working with your client's financial staff, you've projected the cash flows lost because of this infringement. They are (in millions):

Year 1	Year 2	Year 3	Year 4	Year 5
$3.6	$4.3	$5.8	$3.0	$1.7

Using the WACOC of the firm (11.8%) as the discount rate, you can find the present value of each year's lost cash flow. Adding them together, as in Exhibit 4-3, you can determine the total present value of the damages.

THE PROBLEM OF THE PRIVATELY OWNED FIRM

Many legal cases in which cost of capital plays a role involve privately owned firms. Being privately owned, they

Exhibit 4-3.   Finding the Present Value of Damages at a
Discount Rate of 11.8% ($ millions)

PV		1	2	3	4	5	Year
		$3.6	$4.3	$5.8	$3.0	$1.7	Lost cash
3.22							flow
+							
3.44							
+							
4.15							
+							
1.92							
+							
0.97							

$13.70 million

produce no regular trail of stock prices from which betas
can be determined. Nor is there actively traded debt from
which the cost of debt can be estimated. The same problem applies in situations involving a single division of a
multi-division corporation. Likewise, the lack of price information means that both the capital asset pricing model
and the dividend growth model cannot be simply applied.
So how can we determine the cost of equity for these firms?

   One method is to find comparable firms that have
observable betas, and, after making adjustments for key
differences, use their betas as proxies. For example, suppose that Biodyne Corporation is a privately owned firm
for which we cannot determine a market beta. Looking
around the biotech industry we find a publicly traded company, ChromoTech, which is about the same size as
Biodyne and growing at about the same rate. Its beta is

listed as 1.7 by a brokerage firm that provides regular research on the company.

As we know, a company's beta is a measure of the
riskiness (or volatility) of its returns relative to the overall
stock market. Since the beta of the market, by definition,
is 1.0, a 1% change in the market return has been associated with a 1.7% change in the return of ChromoTech stock.

So, can we simply adopt ChromoTech's beta as a
proxy for Biodyne? Probably not; at least not until we adjust for differences in financial leverage between the two
companies.

As we observed in the case of Macy's, the effect of financial leverage on beta and expected return is such that
we cannot use one company's beta as a proxy beta for a
similar company unless we make some adjustment for the
difference in financial leverage. Let's try to make that adjustment in the case of ChromoTech and Biodyne.

First, let's review what we know about these two
similar biotech companies.

Biodyne's beta is the missing value, which may well
be higher than 1.70 because of the company's higher level of
debt. To determine this beta, we first "delever" ChromoTech – in effect, estimating what its beta would be if it
had no debt. We then "relever" the beta using Biodyne's
60% debt-equity ratio, and use the resulting beta as a
proxy for Biodyne.

	Tax rate	Beta	Debt-equity
ChromoTech	40%	1.70	30%
Biodyne	40%	?	60%

To delever ChromoTech, the formula presented in the Macy's case serves our need:

$$\text{ChromoTech } \beta_L = \beta_u \times [1 + (1 - \text{tax rate}) \times \frac{\text{debt}}{\text{equity}}]$$

or

$$1.70 = \beta_u \times [1 + (1 - .40) \times 0.30]$$
$$\beta_u = 1.44.$$

This number makes sense, since the unlevered version of the same firm would naturally have a lower beta.

Now we use this unlevered beta, along with the known tax rate and debt-equity ratio of Biodyne to estimate Biodyne's beta:

$$\begin{aligned}
\text{Biodyne } \beta_L &= \beta_u \times [1 + (1 - \text{tax rate}) \times \frac{\text{debt}}{\text{equity}}] \\
&= 1.44 \times [1 + (1 - .40) \times .60] \\
&= 1.96
\end{aligned}$$

This estimated beta can then be used in calculating Biodyne's cost of equity using the traditional formula:

$$\text{Cost of equity} = \text{risk-free rate} + \beta \times (\text{market premium})$$

Assuming a 6% risk-free rate and a 7% market premium, Biodyne's cost of equity is thus determined to be 19.7%. This can be seen, as follows:

$$.197 = .06 + 1.96(.07)$$

WHAT ABOUT PREFERRED STOCK?

Although not as common as debt or equity, you may occasionally encounter a situation in which shares of preferred stock are part of the capital structure.

Preferred stock is a hybrid form of security, with some characteristics of common stock and some of a bond. Like a bond, it is committed to pay a regular, usually fixed, payment to its holders. But failure to pay this dividend cannot drive the corporation into bankruptcy. And unlike interest payments, dividend payments are not tax-deductible for the corporation. Also, preferred shareholders have preference over common shareholders in the event of bankruptcy. Since preferred shares have no maturity date, they may be thought of as perpetuities.

Besides the standard preferred just described, these securities come in a variety of forms. "Cumulative" preferreds entitle holders to back-payment of dividends in the event that the issuer has missed a payment due to financial distress or other cause. Typically, common shareholders cannot receive any dividends until what is owed to the preferreds has been paid. "Convertible" preferreds are similar to convertible bonds, offering regular payments with the opportunity to convert to common shares according to a predetermined formula. Some preferreds offer "adjustable rate" features that increase or decrease the size of the dividend in response to market interest rates. Still others, "participating preferreds," offer both a regular dividend along with an opportunity to share in the growing fortunes of the issuing corporation.

Like debt and equity, the cost of preferred capital is the minimum cost of inducing an investor to buy or hold the preferred security. That cost is defined by its "dividend yield," or:

$$\text{Cost of preferred capital} = \frac{\text{Dividend}}{\text{Price}}$$

When calculating the cost of capital for a corporation that has debt, common equity, and preferred, simply include the cost of preferred capital, weighted by its percentage of total capital, in the basic equation as follows:

$$\begin{pmatrix} \text{weighted average} \\ \text{cost of capital} \end{pmatrix} = \begin{pmatrix} \text{weight of} \\ \text{debt} \end{pmatrix} \text{x} \begin{pmatrix} \text{cost of} \\ \text{debt} \end{pmatrix}$$

$$+$$

$$\begin{pmatrix} \text{weight of} \\ \text{equity} \end{pmatrix} \text{x} \begin{pmatrix} \text{cost of} \\ \text{equity} \end{pmatrix}$$

$$+$$

$$\begin{pmatrix} \text{weight of} \\ \text{preferred} \end{pmatrix} \text{x} \begin{pmatrix} \text{cost of} \\ \text{preferred} \end{pmatrix}$$

Chapter 5

Valuation

On his sixtieth birthday, your client, Donald Hopkins, is thinking about selling Safeguard Controls, Inc., a small corporation with $10 million in annual revenues. Hopkins owns 40 percent of the company and the remainder is owned by his three brothers. The question is: what is Safeguard Controls actually worth? Don Hopkins has one idea about the company's value; his brothers each have another. Ultimately, they will have to reach some agreement on the value of Safeguard Controls before the four owners can structure a sale of Hopkins' interests.

Agreement on the value of an ongoing business can be elusive. The ongoing business typically owns real property, inventory, productive assets, and, in many cases, patents and receivables. What are these worth? And what are the expectations of future revenues and profits? For public companies like Ford and AT&T, active trading of corporate securities provides some estimate of value. Every day, thousands of investors signal their opinions through the buying and selling of their shares. But for closely-held corporations like Safeguard Controls, there is no public market for ownership, and no daily estimate of company value.

Whether the object of interest is a piece of real property, a share of stock, or an entire company, the question "what is it worth" is extremely important in many situations and commands the attention of attorneys across the country every day. Attorneys regularly find themselves involved in this question in a variety of contexts, including the following situations:

- the purchase or sale of a privately held business
- an estate settlement
- a divorce case
- a buy-sell arrangement between two partners
- an option to buy part of a business
- the sale or purchase of an operating unit of a larger business
- a business considering alternative reorganization plans
- a fraudulent conveyance claim associated with a leveraged buyout

Though the issue of valuation is often encountered by the corporate attorney, few law schools provide adequate training in this complex area of finance.

METHODOLOGIES

A wide range of methodologies has been applied in estimating a firm's value. These include accounting-oriented approaches and the more rigorous discounted cash flow (DCF) analysis based upon the time-value concepts described earlier. Each has unique benefits and drawbacks. None is foolproof. For example, accounting-oriented methods have the virtue of being simple and straightforward, but accounting values often differ from true economic values. DCF analysis, on the other hand, focuses on true economic values but requires the use of *estimated* future cash flows that may or may not prevail, and it requires the choice of discount rates that may be subject to challenge. Different cash flow estimates or discount rates can result in widely different valuations.

This chapter describes several of the commonly used methods for valuing a business, their strengths, and their pitfalls. While our treatment of this subject will not make you an expert, it will help you understand the valuation process and the situations in which certain methodologies may be most appropriate.

BOOK VALUE

The most simple and straightforward approach to the valuation of a company is the use of the book value method, an accounting-oriented approach. The data upon which this value is based is generally easy to obtain. Using this approach, the total value of the firm is the book value of its assets. In order to derive the value of a firm's equity, one merely takes the value of the assets less the liabilities on the company's books. In other words, the residual left after subtracting the firm's book liabilities from its book assets is the value of the company's equity – generally called *Owners'* or *Shareholders' Equity.*

In the case of Brothers Hardware, Inc., a Chicago-based chain of hardware stores described in Exhibit 5-1, we can see that the book value of the company's equity is $13.2 million. This is found by subtracting total liabilities from total assets ($26.1 million less $12.9 million).

The book value method, however, gives a distorted picture of equity value. This distortion has its origin in the accounting values from which it is derived. In the case of Brothers Hardware, two asset categories – property and inventory – may conceal a wide divergence between true economic value and the accounting values represented on the balance sheet. This occurs because accounting practices record assets at their *historical costs.*

Exhibit 5-1. Brothers Hardware, Inc. Balance Sheet
           ($ millions)

Assets			Liabilities		
Cash	$	0.5	Accounts payable	$	0.8
Marketable securities		1.0	Loans payable		0.6
Accounts receivable		0.1	Accrued wages payable		1.0
Inventories		6.5	Accrued taxes payable		1.5
Total current assets	$	8.1	Total current liabilities	$	3.9
			Principal balance		
Gross property		23.0	on mortgage		9.0
Less depreciation		(5.0)			
Net property	$	18.0	Total liabilities		$ 12.9
			Owners' equity		$ 13.2
			Liabilities +		
Total assets		$ 26.1	Owners' equity		$ 26.1

Let's consider the property value first. If the Brothers building had been purchased 12 years ago at $23 million, the value on the firm's books today would be $23 million less any accumulated depreciation. This book value would ignore the fact that the value of this property may have increased dramatically over the past 10 years. If its market value had merely risen by 3% per year over this period, it would be worth $30.9 million today. It is easy to óverlook the powerful effect that changing property values can have on the market value of some companies. Consider the case of companies located in New England, where real estate values nearly tripled in one decade and then plummeted by 20% to 30% in the following years. These wild fluctuations were never reflected in company book values.

Similarly, changes can cause severe distortions in the estimated value of a firm's equipment and inventory. Consider the national retail chains that deployed dozens of electro-mechanical cash registers in each of their many stores. The advent of computerized cash registers caused the market value of their old equipment to drop like a rock. The same happened to record companies whose equipment for manufacturing vinyl records plummeted in value when digital audio tape, then compact disc and successor technologies entered the market.

Now consider the stated value of the Brothers Hardware inventory. Like property value, inventory value is based on historical cost. This ignores the fact that the value of inventory may have changed since it was purchased. Even in the absence of technological obsolescence, inventory is subject to spoilage. Moreover, the inventory cost is typically based on either a first in-first out (FIFO) or a last in-first out (LIFO) costing system. The costing system has nothing to do with which inventory is actually used to fill orders. Just because FIFO is used, for example, does not mean that the first items coming into inventory are actually the first ones to go out of inventory. It is merely an accounting convention to help determine value.

To appreciate how these costing systems can create divergence between accounting and economic values, suppose that the market price of the items in inventory has increased. Under FIFO, if prices are rising, the first items into inventory (the low-cost items) are considered sold first. Therefore, the value of the inventory on the balance sheet reflects the latest items purchased, or the highest cost items. If LIFO is used, again assuming prices are rising, the last items, or highest cost items, are assumed to be the first ones to be sold. The value of inventory on the balance sheet, therefore, reflects the items remaining in the inventory, namely the lowest cost items.

Given the potential disparity between the value of both assets and liabilities recorded on a company's books and their corresponding market values, anyone who adopts a pure book value approach must be prepared to defend a likely attack on the fundamentals of this valuation method.

ADJUSTED BOOK VALUE

The problems inherent in the pure book value method have led to the development of a potentially more realistic valuation approach: the adjusted book value method. While the book value of equity merely considers the historical cost of assets and liabilities, *the adjusted book value restates balance sheet items based on their market values.*

The case of the leveraged buyout (LBO) of Macy's provides an example of how book value and adjusted book value can be dramatically different. Prior to its leveraged buyout, Macy's had a book value of equity amounting to $1.3 billion or $25.87 per share. Yet, at the time, the market value of various line items on its balance sheet were far greater than their historical costs. The market value of inventory, for example, was greater than the stated value on the firm's books. In Exhibit 5-2, the book value of inventory is included in the value of total current assets. To obtain the market value of inventory, it is necessary to add $51.9 million to Macy's book value. Moreover, the book value of property, plant & equipment (PP&E) also had to be adjusted to more appropriately reflect market value. In this example, *replacement value* was used as a market value proxy. In other words, replacing the firm's PP&E would cost $1.823 billion. While replacement costs may not equal the market value of the specific assets deployed by a firm, it is sometimes considered a surrogate, or approximation, when market value data is not readily available.

In addition to these adjustments to book value, there were surplus assets in Macy's pension plan. As a result of these and other adjustments, Macy's adjusted book value of equity was nearly $2.2 billion or $42.67 per share.

Interestingly, as can be seen from the calculation of Macy's adjusted book value, the largest line item was the value of the company's property, plant and equipment. During the recession occurring several years after the Macy's buyout, the value of real estate around the country was significantly reduced, leading to a dramatic reduction of the firm's adjusted book value of equity. In addition to real estate values plummeting, cash flows were also dramatically affected by the recession, resulting in the firm's much publicized bankruptcy.

THE USE OF MULTIPLES IN VALUING A FIRM

An entrepreneur was having lunch with a friend in the investment banking business. "You know," said the entrepreneur, "I've been talking with some local business people about the possibility of buying Community Convenience Stores. It's a fairly small chain, not publicly traded, and does not appear to be very well-run or responsive to the needs of the region. They think it could be much better managed and more profitable. How much do you think it would take to buy the firm."

"How much are its current earnings?" asked the financier.

"Around $500,000."

Exhibit 5-2. Macy's Adjusted Book Value ($ millions)

	Total Current Assets	$	979.0
-	Total Current Liabilities		686.9
=	Working Capital	$	292.1
+	Increased Value of Inventory		51.9
+	Replacement Value of Property, Plant & Equipment		1,823.3
+	Surplus Assets in Pension Plan		93.3
+	Other Assets		283.8
=	Replacement Value of Assets	$	2,544.4
-	Long-Term Debt		134.2
-	Capitalized Leases		50.5
-	Other Liabilities		162.9
=	ADJUSTED BOOK VALUE OF EQUITY	$	2,196.8
÷	Number of Shares (million)		51.5
=	Adjusted Book Value Per Share	$	42.67
	STATED BOOK VALUE OF EQUITY	$	1,332.0
÷	Number of Shares (million)		51.5
=	Stated Book Value Per Share	$	25.87

"I don't know much about the company," said the financier, "but generally, convenience stores of that size in the area are selling at around five times current earnings. So $2.5 million might be a ballpark figure."

The entrepreneur's friend was giving a rough estimate of the value of a business based upon a multiple of its business performance – current net earnings. As we will see in this section, multiples of this kind are often used as a rule-of-thumb for estimating the value of a business.

The value of a company as an ongoing business – and not as a set of separately salable parts – is ultimately determined by its ability to generate a stream of future earnings and cash flows. The greater its ability to expand that stream, the greater its value.

When they buy shares of a company, investors understand that they are not buying the past or the present. They are buying the future. The greater the expectations for future growth in earnings and cash flows, the more the investor is willing to pay. Risk also affects how investors view the value of a firm. The greater the uncertainty associated with a firm's expected earnings or cash flow, the less investors are willing to pay for it. Thus, as risk increases, the firm's multiple is reduced. Unfortunately, the use of multiples is not a standardized procedure. Multiples vary in their definition and the data used to calculate them. To get a sense of how these different measures are derived from a company's financial statements and used to estimate a company's value, consider T&A Fabrications, Inc., a public firm described by Exhibit 5-3.

The following sections use T&A to describe several multiples commonly used by corporate lawyers and litigators.

THE P/E MULTIPLE

We observe the value that investors place on a company through the *multiple* they pay for certain measures of business performance. The most widely used multiple is the P/E or *price-earnings* ratio. This is a ratio of the stock price to the company's current earnings per share, indicating the amount investors are willing to pay for each dollar of current net earnings. For example, a P/E of 10 indicates that investors are paying $10 for each dollar of current net earn-

Exhibit 5-3. T&A Fabrications, Inc. Selected Financial
            Data ($ millions)

		$	10.0
	Sales	$	10.0
-	Cost of Goods Sold		6.5
=	Gross Margin	$	3.5
-	Selling, General and Administrative		1.3
-	Depreciation		0.6
-	Amortization		0.1
-	Interest		0.5
=	Net Profit Before Taxes	$	1.0
-	Taxes (40%)		0.4
=	Net Profit After Taxes	$	0.6

Other Information:

Capital Expenditures	$	0.1
Increase in Working Capital	$	0.1
Long-Term Debt	$	3.0
Total Debt	$	5.0
Market Price Per Share ($ per share)	$	15.00
Number of Shares Outstanding	1 million	

ings. The size of the multiple reveals investors' expectations for future growth. For example, their willingness to
pay $20 or $30 for each dollar of current earnings indicates
their expectation of strong future growth. Evidence confirms that high-growth companies command higher P/E ratios.

Net earnings are the basis for the P/E calculation.
This measure includes the effects of operations, capital
structure (namely, interest payments), and taxes.

Consider the P/E ratio for the publicly held firm T&A Fabrications described in Exhibit 5-3. The company's net profit after taxes was $600,000 and it has one million shares outstanding, indicating earnings per share of $0.60. Thus, the price-earnings ratio can be derived as follows:

$$\frac{P}{E} = \frac{\text{Price per share}}{\text{Earnings per share}} = \frac{\$15}{\$0.60} = 25$$

Obviously, the same ratio could have been derived by dividing the total market value of T&A's equity, $15 million ($15 per share x 1 million shares), by its total earnings, $.6 million.

The P/E ratio, 25, has a number of potential uses. For example, if the firm's earnings are projected to be $1 million five years from now, one might use the ratio to obtain the estimated equity value at that time as $25 million (25 x earnings of $1 million). Clearly, this method assumes that the P/E ratio will not change over the five year interval.

It is important to note that the P/E ratio is used to estimate the value of the firm's equity. If the objective is to obtain the total value of the firm, you must add the firm's debt to its equity value.

Another application of the P/E ratio is the valuation of a privately held firm. Suppose that you want to value the equity of a privately held firm in the same industry as T&A, with reported earnings of $1.5 million. You can use T&A as a surrogate firm and multiply the privately held firm's $1.5 million earnings by T&A's P/E ratio, 25, to obtain an estimated equity value of $37.5 million. Though there are no two firms identical in all respects, the use of a surrogate involves the art of selecting the most appropriate firms to be used as comparables.

THE EBIT MULTIPLE

To determine the value of a firm, analysts often use a multiple based on the firm's earnings before interest and taxes (EBIT). The EBIT is frequently referred to as operating income. The multiple is defined as the total value of the firm divided by its EBIT. The total value of the firm is estimated by adding the value of its equity to its total debt outstanding. EBIT represents the firm's earnings before interest and taxes which, unlike earnings after taxes, are the earnings available to both equity holders in the form of profits and to debt holders to cover the firm's fixed financial obligations. Therefore, while the P/E ratio, which is based on net earnings available to shareholders, is used to determine the value of the firm's equity, the EBIT multiple is used to determine the total value of the firm.

To determine EBIT for the T&A Fabrication example discussed in Exhibit 5-3, the following calculation is performed:

Exhibit 5-4. T&A Fabrications, Inc. EBIT Calculation
($ millions)

	Sales	$10.0
-	Cost of Goods Sold	6.5
-	Selling, General & Administrative	1.3
-	Depreciation	0.6
-	Amortization	0.1
=	EBIT	$ 1.5

Given that the equity is valued at $15 million and that the firm has $5 million in debt, the EBIT multiple can be derived as follows:

$$\frac{\text{Firm Value}}{\text{EBIT}} = \frac{\text{Equity} + \text{Debt}}{\text{EBIT}} = \frac{\$15 \text{ million} + \$5 \text{ million}}{\$1.5 \text{ million}} = 13.3$$

Suppose that T&A's EBIT in five years is expected to increase to $2.5 million. The estimated total value of the firm five years from now is $33.25 million (Value-to-EBIT ratio of 13.3 x projected EBIT of $2.5 million). If five years from now the debt is projected to be $9 million, the projected equity at that time will be equal to $24.25 million (firm value of $33.25 million - debt of $9 million).

Another application of the EBIT multiple is the determination at the present time of either the total value of a privately held firm or the value of the firm's equity. In these situations, you could calculate the EBIT multiple for a firm such as T&A Fabrications and then multiply this value by the EBIT of the privately held firm. For example, by multiplying T&A's multiple of 13.3 and the privately held firm's EBIT of, say, $4.5 million, you would obtain an estimate of $59.85 million (EBIT multiple of 13.3 x EBIT of $4.5 million) for the value of the firm. To determine the value of the privately held firm's equity, you would subtract the total value of its debt, say $10 million, from the firm's value of $59.85 million to obtain an estimate of the value of its equity $49.85 million.

This method is frequently used in both corporate finance and litigation settings. For example, in a recent matter involving the equity valuation of Great Lakes Bus

Lines, the EBIT multiple method was used[1]. First, we identified 15 comparable transactions in the busing industry. For each target, the operating income and the value of the firm's debt plus its equity, often referred to as the Business Enterprise Value, were obtained. In this case, the Business Enterprise Value was provided by Securities Data Corporation (SDC), a firm specializing in providing financial data. Exhibit 5-5 presents the Business Enterprise Value, EBIT and EBIT multiple.

The median EBIT multiple, 13.87, was then multiplied by the most recent year's EBIT of Great Lakes Bus Lines, $7.33 million. The product of the EBIT multiple and the EBIT results in an implied Business Enterprise Value of Great Lakes Bus Lines of $101.67 million. Finally, in order to determine the value of equity, we subtract its debt, $58.99 million, from the estimated enterprise value. This results in an equity value of $42.68 million. The calculation is performed as follows:

	Median Comparable EBIT Multiple	13.87	
x	Great Lakes' EBIT	$ 7.33	million
=	Great Lakes' Business Enterprise Value	$ 101.67	million
-	Great Lakes' Debt	$ 58.99	million
=	Great Lakes' Equity	$ 42.68	million

Unfortunately, the Business Enterprise Value is not uniquely defined. Some consider it to consist of the market value of equity plus total debt. Others use only interest bearing debt. Other definitions are also frequently used. As long as one is consistent in its use, alternative measures of the Business Enterprise Value can be used in analyzing a firm.

---

[1] To maintain confidentiality, the names and numbers associated with the busing companies mentioned in this book have been changed.

Exhibit 5-5. Analysis of EBIT Multiples of Great Lakes'
Comparables ($ millions)

Target Name	Target's Business Enterprise Value	EBIT	EBIT Multiple
Aztec Group	$ 348.37	$ 21.70	16.05
Bordon Bus Lines	71.10	7.36	9.66
Commonwealth Lines	39.04	5.00	7.81
Corcoran Lines	89.20	10.87	8.21
Cross Country Bus Co.	642.75	97.10	6.62
Inter City Lines	38.99	2.75	14.18
Lone Star Bus Co.	159.06	9.30	17.10
McTavish Bus Lines	101.30	2.89	35.05
Minnesota Group	461.60	31.30	14.75
Mountain Transportation	1,161.12	82.00	14.16
Sahara Transportation	686.78	46.40	14.80
Saturn Bus Lines	38.72	8.80	4.40
Southern Transport	25.45	1.87	13.58
Southern Bus Co.	40.03	(0.60)	NMF
Traveler Bus Lines	163.59	13.00	12.58
		MEAN	13.50
		MEDIAN	13.87

Suppose we want to determine the equity value of Doni, Inc., a retail chain specializing in high end retail women's clothing. In step 1, once a list of comparable firms has been obtained, the EBIT multiple is calculated for each firm on the list. The purpose of step 2 is to obtain an estimate of the equity value of Doni. The median or average multiple from step 1 is then multiplied by Doni's EBIT.

The product is an estimate of Doni's Business Enterprise Value. Finally, once Doni's debt is subtracted from Doni's enterprise value, the result is the estimated value of Doni's equity.

The general framework for applying the EBIT multiple is presented as follows:

$$
\text{STEP 1:} \quad \frac{\text{Equity}_{\text{comparable}} + \text{Debt}_{\text{comparable}}}{\text{EBIT}_{\text{comparable}}} = \text{EBIT MULTIPLE}_{\text{comparable}}
$$

$$
\text{STEP 2:} \quad \text{Equity}_{\text{Doni}} = (\text{EBIT MULTIPLE}_{\text{comparable}}) \times \text{EBIT}_{\text{Doni}} - \text{Debt}_{\text{Doni}}
$$

Even though different experts might use different measures of Doni's debt, this does not pose a problem for the determination of the equity value. In other words, as long as the same measure of debt is used in the calculation of the EBIT multiple in step 1 and for Doni's debt value used in step 2, there is no inconsistency.

THE EBITDA MULTIPLE

The EBIT multiple is based on a firm's EBIT or operating earnings. This value is determined after subtracting operating expenses including both depreciation and amortization from the firm's gross profit. Since depreciation and amortization are non-cash expenses, multiples are often calculated based on EBIT plus depreciation and amortization (EBITDA). Similar to the EBIT multiple, the EBITDA multiple is also based on the total value of the firm. Exhibit 5-6 illustrates the calculation of EBITDA for T&A Fabrications.

Exhibit 5-6. T & A Fabrications, Inc. EBITDA Calculation
($ millions)

	Sales	$ 10.0
-	Cost of Goods Sold	6.5
-	Selling, General & Administrative	1.3
-	Depreciation	0.6
-	Amortization	0.1
=	EBIT	$ 1.5
+	Depreciation	0.6
+	Amortization	0.1
=	EBITDA	$ 2.2

The EBITDA multiple can be derived by dividing the firm's value by its EBITDA, as follows:

$$\frac{\text{Firm Value}}{\text{EBITDA}} = \frac{\text{Equity} + \text{Debt}}{\text{EBITDA}} = \frac{\$15 \text{ million} + \$5 \text{ million}}{\$2.2 \text{ million}} = 9.09$$

Like the EBIT multiple, T&A's EBITDA multiple has several potential applications, including the valuation of a privately held company, the valuation of a division of a multidivision firm, or the estimation of the value of a business at a future point in time.

In the same way that the equity of Great Lakes Bus Lines was estimated using the EBIT multiple, another estimate of the value can be obtained using EBITDA. Exhibit 5-7 presents the EBITDA multiple for acquisition targets in Great Lakes' industry. The multiples are derived by dividing each target's Business Enterprise Value by its EBITDA.

Exhibit 5-7. Analysis of EBITDA Multiples of Great
Lakes' Comparables ($ millions)

Target Name	Target's Business Enterprise Value	EBITDA	EBITDA Multiple
Aztec Group	$ 348.37	$ 39.90	8.73
Bordon Bus Lines	71.10	9.52	7.47
Commonwealth Lines	39.04	8.10	4.82
Corcoran Lines	89.20	17.39	5.13
Cross Country Bus Co.	642.75	152.80	4.21
Inter City Lines	38.99	9.03	4.32
Lone Star Bus Co.	159.06	18.70	8.51
McTavish Bus Lines	101.30	23.56	4.30
Minnesota Group	461.60	74.30	6.21
Mountain Transportation	1,161.12	103.03	11.27
Sahara Transportation	686.78	132.80	5.17
Saturn Bus Lines	38.72	15.90	2.44
Southern Transport	25.45	2.87	8.87
Southern Bus Co.	40.03	2.40	16.68
Traveler Bus Lines	163.59	20.80	7.86
		MEAN	7.07
		MEDIAN	6.21

Using the median of the targets' multiples (6.21) and Great Lakes' EBITDA ($13.68 million), the implied value of Great Lakes' business is $84.95 million (multiple of 6.21 x Great Lakes' EBITDA of 13.68). From this value of the enterprise ($84.95 million), you subtract the amount of Great Lakes' debt ($58.98 million) to obtain the value of its equity ($25.97 million).

As illustrated by the Great Lakes example, working with real life numbers differs from textbook examples. This was seen by observing that using both the EBIT and EBITDA multiples, the equity values derived for Great Lakes Bus Lines differed. Using the EBIT multiple, the equity was estimated at $42.68 million, while using the EBITDA multiple, the equity was estimated at $25.97 million. In this litigation, the key concern was the solvency of Great Lakes. Indeed, both multiples result in the firm being solvent by a wide margin.

MULTIPLES: OTHER FACTORS TO CONSIDER

We have reviewed three frequently used multiples. However, there are numerous other multiples used in different situations and different industries. Examples of such multiples include price/revenue and price/book value. Moreover, measures of value within an industry are often based on industry specific multiples. Frequently, one sees multiples based on operating measures such as revenue per square foot, tonnage, or yields. In addition, multiples may require adjustments to account for industry specific characteristics such as capacity utilization, regulatory climate and intensity of foreign competition. Under certain conditions, company specific adjustments are warranted. Examples of such adjustments include the company's market share, its geographic location and the quality of its management. In addition, for closely held businesses, a discount from public company multiples is often taken to reflect the lack of marketability of the company shares.

While some multiples are based on EBIT or EBITDA, which are determined before tax, others are calculated on an after-tax basis. Finally, an issue which is often argued in litigation is the time period to be used for the numerator and denominator of the multiple. For example, in the case of Great Lakes Bus Lines, we were asked to value the firm as of April. An important issue was whether we should use the most recent 12 months of data available (which was based on internal management reports), or the most recent audited financial reports. The decision as to which financials to use should be based on which ones best reflect the firm's ordinary operations.

Multiples are not used solely to determine value, but also to determine whether a public company's market value is high or low relative to other firms in the same industry. Exhibit 5-8 compares the price/EBIT multiple paid by various acquirers for targets in the entertainment industry. For example, consider the multiple paid by Sony Corporation for its acquisition of Columbia Pictures. As indicated by the exhibit, Columbia's purchase price-to-EBIT multiple of 23.4 was significantly higher than those of all others listed.

With the benefit of hindsight, we know that Sony's expectations never materialized. Five years after the acquisition, Sony wrote off $2.7 billion in losses from its high-priced takeover. Interestingly, Pathe Communications' takeover of MGM/UA, seen at the bottom of the acquisition chart, fared no better. The takeover was followed by year after year of MGM losses. These losses, and the lack of capital, prevented it from producing the industry average 20 films per year or making the investments needed to produce a positive cash flow. So, potential problems may arise both at the top and bottom of the chart.

Exhibit 5-8. Movie Industry Stock Purchase-to-EBIT Multiple

Target *Acquirer*	Stock Purchase Price-to-EBIT
Columbia Picture Entertainment *Sony Corporation*	23.4
MCA Inc. *Matsushita Electric Industrial*	14.4
Orion Pictures *Metromedia Co.*	8.7
Twentieth Century Fox *News Corporation Ltd.*	8.3
Lorimar Inc. *Telepictures Corporation*	8.2
New World Entertainment *Andrews Group Inc.*	(1.6)*
Lorimar Telepictures *Warner Communications*	(10.0)
Guber-Peters Entertainment Co. *Sony Corporation*	(11.6)
MGM/UA Communications *Pathe Communications*	(122.1)

* The negative ratios of the last four enterprises result from negative earnings

They may occur at the top as a result of paying too high a multiple, or at the bottom if the expectations for a turn-around do not materialize.

CAPITALIZATION OF DIVIDENDS AND CASH FLOWS

The value of a firm increases as the growth rates of projected dividends and operating cash flows increase.   For
example, consider two firms – A and B – with the same
number of shares outstanding.   Each has an annual dividend of $1.50 per share.   The difference between these
firms is that A's dividend is expected to grow at 10% per
year while B's expected growth is only 3% per year.   Exhibit
5-9 projects the dividends for the coming year and the following four years.   It should be clear that the expectation of
higher future dividends makes Firm A more valuable, all
other factors being equal. And what holds for future dividends holds true for future earnings and future cash flow,
even if they are not distributed to the owners.   If they are
not distributed, there is the very real presumption that
earnings or cash flows will be reinvested in the business,
creating the potential for greater distributions in the future.

Exhibit 5-9.   Dividend Projections

Year	1	2	3	4	5
Firm A (growth rate 10%)	1.50	1.65	1.82	2.00	2.20
Firm B (growth rate 3%)	1.50	1.55	1.59	1.64	1.69

To use the capitalization approach, one typically assumes that after a certain point in time, the growth rate of
dividends will continue unabated at a constant rate.   These
dividends are discounted back to the present.   Since dividends flow directly to shareholders, they are discounted

back to the present using the shareholders' required rate of return, often referred to as the *cost of equity*. This framework can be simplified using the following relationship, known as the Gordon Dividend Model:

$$\text{Current Value of Equity} = \frac{\text{Coming Year's Dividends}}{\text{Cost of Equity - Growth Rate of Dividends}}$$

For example, for Firm A, above, if we assume that the cost of equity is 14%, then the current value of equity would be:

$$\frac{1.50}{.14-.10} = \frac{1.50}{.04} = \$37.50$$

In this framework, the capitalization rate is the cost of equity less the dividend growth rate, or 4%. In other words, the greater the cost of equity, the smaller the equity value; and the greater the dividend growth rate, the greater the equity value. Moreover, to determine the value of equity at the present time, the capitalization rate is applied to the projected dividends over the next twelve month period.

The capitalization of cash flow approach is similar. The share price is based on the expected cash flows over the coming year, the growth rate of the cash flows, and the appropriate discount rate. Unlike the capitalization of dividends approach, the relevant cash flow is that available to both debt and equity holders. Therefore, the required rate of return is the weighted average rate of return required by both debt and equity holders, commonly referred to as the *weighted average cost of capital*.

THE WEIGHTED AVERAGE COST OF CAPITAL

The cost of capital was extensively discussed in the previous chapter. However, given its significance for valuation, a short review is warranted.

We traditionally describe the *cost of debt* as the firm's cost of borrowing funds. The *cost of equity* is the rate of return the firm's shareholders expect to earn on their investment. Risk plays a big part in both of these costs. The riskier, or less certain, the dividends or cash flows of the firm, the higher the rates that lenders or bond-holders will expect on the firm's IOUs. Likewise, the rate of return expectation of shareholders corresponds to the risk, or uncertainty, associated with future cash flows or dividends.

To find the weighted average cost of capital for a firm, we simply sum two values: the after-tax cost of debt multiplied by the percentage of debt in the firm's capital structure assets, and the cost of equity multiplied by the percentage of equity in its capital structure.

Example: The capital of Williston Corporation is 40% borrowed funds (at a 6% after-tax interest rate) and 60% shareholders equity. Shareholders expect a 15% rate of return.

Weighted Average Cost of Capital for Williston Corp. =
$$.40(.06) + .60(.15) = 11.4\%$$

One key difference between the capitalization of dividends and the capitalization of operating cash flow is the meaning of the resulting value. The dividends solely accrue to shareholders and, as a result, their capitalization reflects the value of the firm's equity. Since the cash flows accrue to both debt holders and equity holders, the capitalized cash flows result in the Business Enterprise Value. As we saw earlier in this chapter, this represents the value of the firm's debt plus its equity. Or in other words, from this value, the firm's debt is subtracted to obtain the value of equity. This valuation framework can be summarized as follows:

$$\text{Business Enterprise Value} = \frac{\text{Projected Debt Free Cash Flow}}{\text{Cost of Capital - Growth Rate of Cash Flow}}$$

$$\text{Value of Equity = Business Enterprise Value - Debt}$$

To understand the nature of these relationships, consider a firm with the following characteristics:

Projected dividends in the coming year	$500 thousand
Projected cash flow in the coming year	$1 million
Projected long-term growth rate of dividends	6%
Projected long-term growth rate of cash flow	6%
Cost of equity	15%
Weighted average cost of capital	12%
Debt	$11.1 million

$$\text{Value of Equity} = \frac{\$500,000}{.15-.06} = \$5.6 \text{ million}$$

$$\text{Business Enterprise Value} = \frac{\$1,000,000}{.12-.06} = \$16.7 \text{ million}$$

Value of Equity = $16.7 million - $11.1 million = $5.6 million

DISCOUNTED CASH FLOW METHODOLOGY

In Chapter 2, we learned about the concept of *present value.* The present value was defined as *the current worth of an amount to be received in the future.* This is a powerful concept in estimating the value of a business. In effect, in finding the current worth of all expected amounts to be received by the owners in the future, we also estimate the value of the business.

To understand this valuation concept, let's first consider a fanciful story. Imagine that you are offered a machine capable of printing real, legitimate money! The machine is guaranteed to print $1.5 million by the end of the first year, another $2 million by the end of the second year, and a growing volume thereafter, as shown in Exhibit 5-10. At the end of the fifth year, the machine will explode, producing no further revenues. This is just what you have always wanted – a machine that will literally print money!

But there is a hitch – the person offering this one-of-a-kind machine expects something in return. The question is, how much is it worth to you? One way to determine the machine's value to you is to discount each of the future amounts to the present and add them together. Thus, the name "Discounted Cash Flow Method."

Recalling what we learned about the present value of a future sum, we recognize that the annual amounts to be printed by the machine represent a set of future values (FV). To find the present value (PV) of each, we need to select an appropriate discount rate (i).

When discounting future dividends to value a business, the discount rate is the *cost of equity*, or the rate of return that the owners require from their investment. In our example, we decide to use 10% as the cost of equity.

Exhibit 5-10. Finding the Present Value of Future
Amounts (discounted at 10% and in
$ millions)

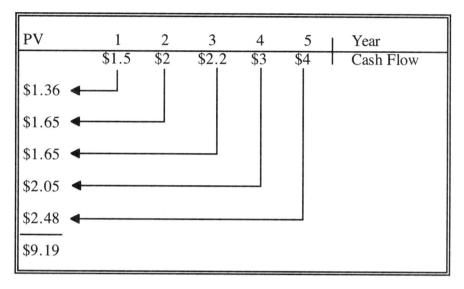

PV	1	2	3	4	5	Year
	$1.5	$2	$2.2	$3	$4	Cash Flow
$1.36						
$1.65						
$1.65						
$2.05						
$2.48						
$9.19						

The future values in the exhibit are easily discounted to the present using the table method shown in
Chapter 2, or by means of a financial calculator. The sum
of these five present values is $9.19 million. This is what
the magic money machine is worth if your cost of money is
10%. In other words, if your client pays $9.19 million for
the machine, he earns exactly 10% on his investment. If
his objective is to earn more than 10%, he has to get his
lawyer to negotiate a purchase price lower than $9.19 mil-
lion.

While our story may seem farfetched, it provides a
simple and direct illustration of the discounted cash flow
(DCF) method. Unlike the accounting-oriented valuation
methods described earlier, the DCF approach is based
upon real economic values, not values subject to accounting
sleights of hand. Further, it recognizes the fact that a
business, like our magic money machine, creates economic

value *over time*. And the DCF approach is constructed in a way that captures value over time, recognizing that the present value of future cash flows decreases as a function of time.

Determining the "terminal value" of a business. Unlike the money-printing machine described in the last example, a business does not explode at the end of five years. In most cases, the business will continue creating economic value for its owners for many years to come. And these future values will increase the present value of the business. But how do we deal with them in estimating the value of the business today? One way is to estimate what we could sell the business for at the end of the fifth year. This sale price would become a future value, which we would discount to the present like any other cash flow.

But how can we estimate what the business will be worth five years from now? One way is to estimate the cash flows to be received in years 6, 7, 8, and so forth. A simpler way is to use a formula for determining the present value of a perpetual series of equal cash flows.

This formula is:

$$\text{Net Present Value} = \frac{\text{Cash Flow}}{\text{Discount Rate}}$$

Thus, if we figured that our money-printing machine would continue to produce $4 million per year forever, and our required rate of return continued to be 10%, then the machine would have the following value when we sold it at the end of year 5:

$$\text{Net Present Value} = \frac{\$4 \text{ million}}{0.10} = \$40 \text{ million}$$

As can be seen in Exhibit 5-11, this "terminal value" of our cash machine is then added to our cash flow in year 5, discounted to the present, and added to the $9.19 million we determined earlier.

As this exhibit indicates, the present value of the $40 million terminal value is $24.84 million, increasing the total present value of the money printing machine to $34.03.

Cash flows are the thing. Unlike the money machine in our story, a business produces more than currency; it generates revenues, operating expenses, depreciation, interest expense and – eventually – accounting earnings or losses. Knowing what to discount in determining value could be a puzzle. The solution to the puzzle is to identify and discount the true economic values generated by the business. These economic values are found in the cash flows of the company.

"Cash flow" is one of the least understood concepts in finance. In essence, it is the after-tax cash from operations available to pay dividends to shareholders and interest to creditors. As such, operating cash flows are often referred to as *debt-free* cash flows.

Determining the present value of these debt-free cash flows results in the same Business Enterprise Value we saw earlier in the chapter. Like earlier, it represents the firm's debt plus its equity. In other words, the Business Enterprise Value can be calculated as follows:

Business Enterprise Value (BEV) = The present value of the firm's future operating cash flows discounted at its cost of capital.

Exhibit 5-11. The Present Value of the Money Printing
Machine ($ millions)

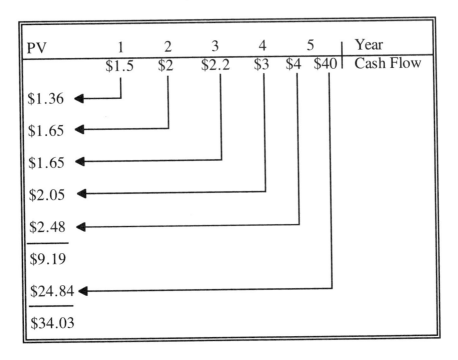

Most businesses are financed by both shareholders' equity
and borrowed funds, or debt. If we are interested in the
value of the firm's equity, we would subtract the firm's debt
from its Business Enterprise Value:

Value of Equity = Business Enterprise Value - Debt

Typically, the cash flow calculation begins with net
income – an accounting measure. Several adjustments are
made to transform this accounting measure into a measure
of economic value, including:

1. Though capital expenditures reduce available cash, they do not pass through the income statement and therefore are not reflected in net income. As a result, in calculating cash flows, capital expenditures should be subtracted from net income. For example, a manufacturer may have spent $5 million on a new factory, but since this is a capital expenditure and not an operating expense (like labor, materials, and so forth), the $5 million has no immediate impact on net income.

2. Changes in working capital (current assets less current liabilities) affect the cash available for distribution to shareholders and debtholders. But, like capital expenditures, it is not reflected in the net income figure. For example, increasing working capital, such as inventory or accounts receivable, reduces cash flow. Similarly, decreasing working capital increases cash flow. However, neither affects bottom line net income.

3. Net income includes a number of non-cash items such as depreciation, amortization, and deferred taxes. These must be added back to net income to obtain cash flow. When accountants calculate net income, they subtract *all* expenses, including these non-cash items, from revenues. These subtractions have the effect of reducing accounting net income. This reduction in actual income is fine for reducing taxable income, but it understates the actual cash flows of the firm. So, to determine cash flow, we must *add back* each of the non-cash items to net income.

4. Since we are interested in the firm's cash flow available to both debt and equity holders, interest payments to creditors should not be subtracted when calculating debt-free cash flows. This has the effect of causing the firm's operating cash flow to be greater than its calculated net in-

come by its interest expense. There are two reasons for excluding interest payments. The first is inherent in the mathematics of discounting: the cost of money is already taken into account by the virtue of discounting future cash flows. The second reason has to do with the outsider's perspective on business valuation. Interest payments are strictly a function of how the current owner has decided to finance the business. Had it been financed entirely with the owner's capital, there would be no interest expense; on the other hand, if some part of the financing came from creditors, an interest charge must be paid by the owner. The economic value created by the company is the same in both cases. Thus, since initially interest is netted out to arrive at net income, it must be added back to obtain the debt-free cash flow.

Note: In adding back interest expense to net income, it is important to add back only the amount of interest paid on an *after-tax* basis. For example, if $1,000 of interest is paid, but the firm's tax rate is 40%, the actual amount of interest paid is $600, or (1 - .40)($1000). Thus, only $600 of interest is added back, not $1000.

To summarize, debt-free cash flow is calculated as follows:

Determination of Debt-Free Cash Flow
Net Income
+   Non-Cash Expenses
-     Capital Expenditures
-     Increases in Working Capital
+   Decreases in Working Capital
=   Free Cash Flow
+   (1 - Tax Rate) x Interest Payments
=   Debt Free Cash Flow

THE DISCOUNTED CASH FLOW METHOD IN ACTION

A recent fraudulent conveyance case required the valuation of a particular company. Here, the goal was to determine whether FoodNut was solvent or insolvent at the time it was purchased through a leveraged buyout – i.e., to determine if the value of the firm's equity was positive (solvent) or negative (insolvent). This case provides an opportunity to demonstrate the application of the DCF method to a valuation problem.

The first step in this analysis is to determine the free cash flow. Once this is known, after-tax interest expense is added back – resulting in debt-free cash flow. Let's go through the analysis step-by-step.

Finding free cash flow. The derivation of the free cash flow is presented in Exhibit 5-12. As indicated by the exhibit, the calculation begins with a projection of the firm's net income for fiscal years 1 through 5. All projected non-cash expenses, such as depreciation, deferred taxes and amortization are then added back to net income. This total constitutes all the sources of cash expected to be generated by the firm. Some of this cash is expected to be allocated to three primary purposes: capital expenditures, changes in working capital and changes in other assets. The total uses are then subtracted from the total sources of cash to obtain FoodNut's free cash flow through year 5.

Debt-free cash flow. Once the free cash flow is determined, the after-tax interest expense is added back. This expense is obtained through the following equation: (1- tax rate) x interest expense. The result of this addition is the

Exhibit 5-12. FoodNut, Inc. Projected Cash Flows

	Year 1	Year 2	($000s) Year 3	Year 4	Year 5
SOURCES OF CASH					
Net Income	$ (2,150)	$(1,195)	$ 1,678	$ 4,843	$ 8,542
Depreciation	491	751	814	883	956
Deferred Taxes	(28)	114	150	162	157
Goodwill Amortization	3,486	3,486	3,486	3,486	3,486
Acquisition Fee Amortization	1,195	1,195	1,195	1,195	1,195
Total Sources	$ 2,994	$ 4,351	$ 7,323	$ 10,569	$14,336
USES OF CASH					
Capital Expenditures	$ 1,200	$ 1,200	$ 1,200	$ 1,200	$ 1,200
Increase (Decrease) in other assets	446	815	703	756	838
Changes in Components of Working Capital:					
Accounts Receivable	363	183	212	227	263
Inventory	1,329	791	683	734	814
Other Current Assets	(801)	195	169	181	201
Accounts Payable	(326)	(893)	(770)	(828)	(918)
Other Current Liabilities	(538)	(231)	(200)	(215)	(238)
Net Change in Working Capital	$ 27	$ 45	$ 94	$ 99	$ 122
Total Uses	$ 1,673	$ 2,060	$ 1,997	$ 2,055	$ 2,160
FREE CASH FLOW	$ 1,321	$ 2,291	$ 5,326	$ 8,514	$12,176

debt-free cash flow of the firm. As can be seen in Exhibit 5-13, the values of debt-free cash flow during the projection period (5 years) range from $7 million to $21.1 million.

But, what about cash flows beyond year 5? Since the organization is expected to be in business past year 5, it is important to obtain a value reflecting the cash flows extending beyond the 5-year horizon. To obtain this value, it is assumed that the year 5 debt-free cash flow of $21.2 million will continue to grow at a constant rate of 4% per year. This reflects a conservative estimate of the firm's long-term growth rate.

Exhibit 5-13. FoodNut, Inc. Debt-Free Cash Flow
             ($ millions)

	Year 1	Year 2	Year 3	Year 4	Year 5
I. Free Cash Flow	$ 1.3	$ 2.3	$ 5.3	$ 8.5	$ 12.2
Interest Expense	$ 9.5	$ 17.2	$ 16.8	$ 16.0	$ 14.8
x (1 - Tax Rate)	60%	60%	60%	60%	60%
II. After-Tax Interest	5.7	10.3	10.1	9.6	8.9
I+II. Debt-Free Cash Flow (Years 1-5)	$ 7.0	$ 12.6	$ 15.4	$ 18.1	$ 21.1

The formulation used to grow the cash flows following year 5 and to discount the resulting values back to year
5 is identical to the capitalized cash flow approach.   In
other words, the value in year 5 of all future cash flows is
year 6's cash flow capitalized at the cost of capital minus
the growth rate. In this case, the firm's weighted average
cost of capital was 13.4% and the growth rate of cash flows
was projected to be 4%. Thus, the present value as of year
5 of all future cash flows expected to be generated in the
years following year 5 is:

$$\frac{21.1(1+.04)}{.134-.04} = \$233.4 \text{ million}$$

We now have an estimate for FoodNut's debt-free
cash flows for years 1 - 5 and beyond. These can be seen in
Exhibit 5-14. Using the DCF methodology and the firm's
cost of capital as the discount rate (13.4%), we can discount
each of them to the present, and by adding them together
obtain the total present value of the firm's debt-free cash
flows, which is $173.3 million. Subtracting the firm's long-

term debt of $129.9 million gives us the firm's equity value: $43.4 million.

Exhibit 5-14. Calculating the Value of FoodNut's Equity
            ($ millions)

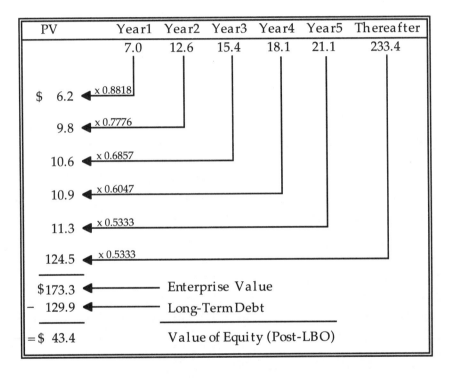

PV		Year1	Year2	Year3	Year4	Year5	Thereafter
		7.0	12.6	15.4	18.1	21.1	233.4
$ 6.2	x 0.8818						
9.8	x 0.7776						
10.6	x 0.6857						
10.9	x 0.6047						
11.3	x 0.5333						
124.5	x 0.5333						
$173.3	Enterprise Value						
− 129.9	Long-Term Debt						
= $ 43.4	Value of Equity (Post-LBO)						

So in this case, the firm had a positive equity value at the time the LBO transaction took place.

Chapter 6

Damages

Damages have traditionally represented the dollar amount necessary to compensate an injured individual or commercial party. For individuals, such compensatory damages generally have amounted to the lost earning capacity of the individual and any associated costs, such as medical care or pain and suffering. These cases typically arise from personal injury situations or from wrongful death. In addition, the plaintiff's bar is increasingly suing for *hedonic* damages, which place a value on the loss of the enjoyment of life.

Damages are also associated with a broad spectrum of commercial cases. They include contract violations, security manipulation, patent infringement, antitrust cases, and many others. While the bulk of commercial cases focus on compensatory damages, a well-publicized minority involve punitive damages. These damages are typically assessed to punish the liable party and prevent it and others from engaging in similar behavior in the future.

The essence of compensatory damages is to restore the wronged party to the financial position he or she would have been in had the wrong not occurred. In other words, compensatory damages aim to make the wronged party whole. In the case of a wrongful death, this means replacing the lost earning power of the deceased, which must be carefully calculated. Lost earning power would typically include the value of the earnings that would have been generated over the remainder of the victim's working life. In a typical commercial damages case, the lost earnings over the period in which the firm was damaged are determined.

A large number of well-publicized damage awards have been made over the past few years. For example, a jury returned a $2.9 million award against McDonald's Corporation, which included $2.7 million in punitive damages. This award, later reduced to $480,000 by a judge, was the result of a 79 year old customer being scalded by coffee served by a McDonald's franchise. In a case against General Motors, an elderly couple won $8 million, claiming their Oldsmobile Delta 88 seat belt was faulty. A 65 year old woman won $24.2 million in a judgment against United Airlines stemming from injuries sustained in the DC-10 crash near Sioux City, Iowa. A federal judge awarded $3.5 million to a 71 year old diabetic who alleged his legs were amputated because of negligent treatment at a veterans hospital. In a sexual harassment suit, a legal secretary won $7.1 million. And in the largest punitive verdict ever, the case of the Exxon Valdez resulted in a $5 billion award. This was in addition to $287 million in compensatory damages.

Less well-publicized than these large damage awards is the fact that half of them are either reversed or reduced by juries or judges.

This chapter provides a general framework for damage calculations, illustrating three types of damages: wrongful death, lost earnings as a result of commercial violations, and securities cases. For each of these situations, a methodology is presented for determining an appropriate damage award.

WRONGFUL DEATH

To determine the compensatory damages associated with a wrongful death, it is necessary to estimate the lost earnings of the victim. In other words, we calculate what the victim would have earned had he lived. This income is estimated for each year of the victim's expected working life. Each year's projected income is then discounted to its present value, and those present values are summed to determine the total present value of the victim's lost income. The method for calculating these present values was explained earlier, in Chapter 2.

Exhibit 6-1 presents each step of the process, as well as a graphic presentation of a method used to determine the present value of the victim's earnings.

The income projections are typically based on either the rate of growth of the victim's own income, or on government statistics relating to historical income growth of individuals with similar demographic characteristics (e.g. race, sex, etc.). The analysis is sometimes performed in *real* terms – i.e., in terms reduced to account for the effects of inflation – and sometimes in *nominal* terms. Nominal terms make no inflation adjustment.

The real earnings growth rate, the nominal earnings growth rate, and the inflation rate are inextricably linked. The nominal growth rate is the real growth rate compounded at the rate of inflation. For example, if the victim's actual (nominal) earnings had been growing at 5%

Exhibit 6-1. The Wrongful Death Methodology in a
           Nutshell

Step 1. Using historical wage growth rate for the victim and/or for the economy in general, estimate the victim's expected earnings for each year that he would have worked, were it not for his untimely death.

Step 2. Determine an appropriate rate for discounting these future earnings to their present values.

Step 3. Calculate the present value of each year's earnings.

Step 4. Sum the present value of each year's earnings.

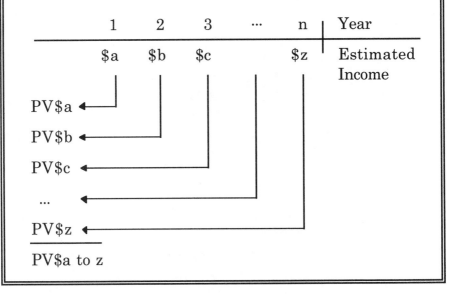

per year, and the rate of inflation had been 4% per year, the real growth would have been:

[1]

$$(1 + \text{Nominal growth rate}) = \left(1 + \begin{matrix}\text{Real growth}\\ \text{rate}\end{matrix}\right)\left(1 + \begin{matrix}\text{Inflation}\\ \text{rate}\end{matrix}\right)$$

$$(1 + .05) = (1 + \text{Real growth rate})(1 + .04)$$

$$1 + \text{Real growth rate} = \frac{1.05}{1.04} = 1.0096$$

$$\text{Real growth rate} = 0.96\%$$

The *real* annual growth rate of the victim's earnings is thus 0.96%. Sometimes, rather than using [1], the following simplified relationship is used:

$$\text{Nominal growth rate} = \left(\begin{matrix}\text{Real growth}\\ \text{rate}\end{matrix}\right) + \left(\begin{matrix}\text{Inflation}\\ \text{rate}\end{matrix}\right)$$

Transposing this equation, we see that:

[2]

$$\begin{aligned}\text{Real growth rate} &= \text{Nominal growth rate - Inflation rate}\\ &= 5\% - 4\%\\ &= 1\%\end{aligned}$$

While 0.96% is the real growth rate obtained by the explicit calculation in [1], an almost identical value of 1% is obtained by using the simplification in [2]. Though the simplification provides a reliable estimate in this situation, it is less reliable in an environment of high inflation or high real growth.

WRONGFUL DEATH EXAMPLE

To integrate the elements just discussed in determining lost earnings, let's consider a typical situation of wrongful death. The victim in this case is John Monroe, age 49, who was killed because of a faulty latch on an amusement park ride. Mr. Monroe was a self-employed electrician.

Step 1: Estimate projected real earnings. Based on previous tax returns, Mr. Monroe's income increased from $17,932 during the first year of self-employment to $29,937 in the last complete year prior to his death. A plot of his historical earnings can be seen in Exhibit 6-2.

Exhibit 6-2. Schedule of Annual Earnings of J. Monroe as a Self-Employed Electrician

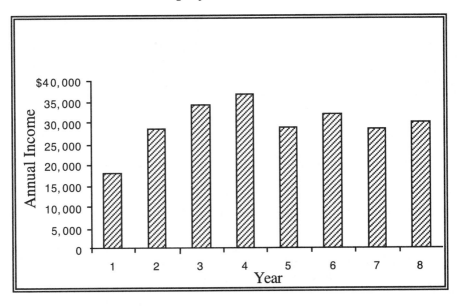

The rate of growth of Mr. Monroe's income from $17,932 to $29,937 during this eight year period was 7.6% per year.

Note: If you have a financial calculator, the growth rate in this case can be easily determined. Just enter Year 1 earnings of $17,932 as the PV (you will need to change the "sign" to negative); enter Year 8 earnings ($29,937) as FV; there this a span of 7 compounding periods here, so enter 7 as n. These steps completed, enter i (or "compute" i, or whatever your particular calculator requires). This will give you the annual percentage growth rate (7.6%).

Yet, as can be seen, his income was initially trending upward, with small year-to-year changes in the recent past. Rather than relying completely on his earnings record to calculate damages, the rate of earnings growth in the economy was also obtained from statistics compiled by the U.S. Department of Labor. Based on these statistics, economy-wide, the *real* rate of earnings growth (i.e., adjusted for inflation) during the 20 year period prior to his death was 0.45%. We will use this real rate of U.S. earnings growth as the basis for projecting Mr. Monroe's earnings into future years. But first, we need to estimate his income for the balance of the calendar year in which he died, which we call Year 1.

Mr. Monroe's death occurred on August 16th, 62.5% through the calendar year. In the year prior to his death, Mr. Monroe's income was $29,937. In estimating his real income for the balance of the year of his death – or Year 1 – we make the assumption that his income will be held con-

Exhibit 6-3. John Monroe's Projected Real Earnings

Year	Projected Earnings to Age 65	Projected Earnings to Age 70
1	$ 11,226.38*	$ 11,226.38*
2	30,071.72	30,071.72
3	30,207.04	30,207.04
4	30,342.97	30,342.97
5	30,479.51	30,479.51
6	30,616.67	30,616.67
7	30,754.45	30,754.45
8	30,892.84	30,892.84
9	31,031.86	31,031.86
10	31,171.50	31,171.50
11	31,311.78	31,311.78
12	31,452.68	31,452.68
13	31,594.22	31,594.22
14	31,736.39	31,736.39
15	31,879.20	31,879.20
16	31,830.52**	32,022.66
17		32,166.76
18		32,311.51
19		32,456.91
20		32,602.97
21		32,553.18***
Total Projected Earnings	$ 476,599.73	$ 638,883.20

* Year 1 income is held constant from the year prior to death. This figure represents 37.5% (or 100%-62.5%) of the year remaining since the time of death.
**99.4% of year 16. Since Mr. Monroe was born on Dec. 29th, projecting his income through age 65 brings the projections through Dec. 29th of the 16th year following his death.
***99.4% of year 21. Since Mr. Monroe was born on Dec. 29th, projecting his income through age 70 brings the projections through Dec. 29th of the 21st year following his death.

stant from the prior year at $29,937. Thus, the income for the remaining portion of that year is determined to be (1 - 0.625) x $29,937, or $11,226.38. For all subsequent years, the projections of his earnings are based on a real growth rate of 0.45%. We then project those real earnings for each year through age 70. In this analysis we develop two earn-ings scenarios: one in which Mr. Monroe works until the normal retirement age of 65, and another to age 70. Since many self-employed persons work past normal retirement age, this second scenario is not unreasonable. The two earnings projections are presented in Exhibit 6-3.

Step 2: Determine the discount rate. Damages are determined by the present value of Mr. Monroe's lost earnings. Since these lost earnings are determined on a real rather than a nominal basis, the discount rate used to obtain the present value must also be calculated on a real basis – without the inflation component that discount rates normally contain.

Economists often use a government bond rate to discount cash flows in wrongful death cases. However, since that rate is typically quoted on a nominal basis, it must be adjusted to derive the real rate. Fortunately, information on both the government bond rate and the inflation rate over many years is readily available. According to published data compiled by Ibbotson & Associates, the long-term compound annual rate on the bonds is 4.8% while the compound annual rate of inflation over the same period has been 3.1%.[1] Thus, the real rate of interest is 1.7% (4.8%-3.1%). This is the rate at which we discount John Monroe's estimated future earnings.

Step 3: Calculate the present value of lost earnings. Now that John Monroe's real earnings have been estimated for each year of what would have been his natural working life, and the discount rate has been determined, we can calculate the present value of his lost earnings. First, however, let us consider the time line associated with the damage calculation.

---

[1] Source: © *Stocks, Bonds, Bills, and Inflation 1995 Yearbook™*, Ibbotson Associates, Chicago, (annually updates work by Roger G. Ibbotson and Rex A. Sinquefield). Used with permission. All rights reserved.

Exhibit 6-4. Damage Time Line

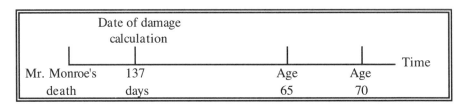

The damage calculation is performed as of the end of the year of Mr. Monroe's death. This is 137 days following his death. For the sake of illustration, the earnings for these 137 days, $11,226.38, are not compounded since they are generated immediately prior to the date of the damage calculation. From the calculation date going forward, each year's projected real earnings is discounted back to the date of the calculation – the end of year 1.

For example, consider the discounted value of the real earnings generated in year 2. This is obtained by discounting year 2's real earnings, $30,071.72, back to the date of the calculation at the discount rate of 1.7%. Using a financial calculator, we solve for PV, using 1 year for n (the number of periods we are discounting), $30,071.72 for FV (the future value), and 1.7 for i (the interest rate). Enter these variables by the procedure used with your particular calculator, and the value for PV (present value) will be: $29,569.05.

Follow this procedure for each year's estimated earnings, add them together, and you will have the total present value of Mr. Monroe's lost earnings. Exhibit 6-5 indicates the total present value of these lost earnings to age 65, and to age 70. At a glance, we see that the present value of Mr. Monroe's lost earnings span a range from $418,412 to $538,251, depending on how late in life we assume he would have worked.

Exhibit 6-5. Present Value of Lost Earnings

Year	Projected Earnings to Age 65	Present Value of Projected Earnings	Projected Earnings to Age 70	Present Value of Projected Earnings
1	$11,226.38	$11,226.38	$11,226.38	$11,226.38
2	30,071.72	29,569.05	30,071.72	29,569.05
3	30,207.04	29,205.61	30,207.04	29,205.61
4	30,342.97	28,846.64	30,342.97	28,846.64
5	30,479.51	28,492.08	30,479.51	28,492.08
6	30,616.67	28,141.89	30,616.67	28,141.89
7	30,754.45	27,796.00	30,754.45	27,796.00
8	30,892.84	27,454.35	30,892.84	27,454.35
9	31,031.86	27,116.91	31,031.86	27,116.91
10	31,171.50	26,783.61	31,171.50	26,783.61
11	31,311.78	26,454.42	31,311.78	26,454.42
12	31,452.68	26,129.26	31,452.68	26,129.26
13	31,594.22	25,808.11	31,594.22	25,808.11
14	31,736.39	25,490.90	31,736.39	25,490.90
15	31,879.20	25,177.59	31,879.20	25,177.59
16	31,830.52	24,718.92	32,022.66	24,868.13
17			32,166.76	24,562.47
18			32,311.51	24,260.57
19			32,456.91	23,962.38
20			32,602.97	23,667.86
21			32,553.18	23,236.70
Total	$476,599.73		$638,883.20	

Present Value of Lost Earnings	$418,411.72		$538,250.91

While this approach was based on the use of real projected earnings and real interest rates, the analysis could have been performed using nominal values of both projected earnings and interest rates. The resulting present values, whether calculated using nominal values or real values, are identical.

Although some states use other approaches, discounting future lost earnings is the most frequently used methodology to determine an individual's lost earning capacity. The analysis presented above did not incorporate either the effects of taxes or personal consumption. Based on statutes and court decisions, their inclusion varies from state to state.

BUSINESS DAMAGES

The objective of business damages is to return the damaged firm to the financial position it would have been in had it not been wronged. In a case involving business damages, it is necessary to determine the economic value that would have accrued to the wronged firm in the absence of the wrong. In most cases, these values will have accrued over a number of years – past and future. Time value of money methodologies drawn from Chapter 2 help us determine them.

The quest for economic contribution. In the previous section, we estimated the future earnings of the victim of a wrongful death. In the case of business damages, we again attempt to state what earnings *would have been* in the absence of a certain event – here, a contract violation. The stated earnings of a business firm, however, may not be a true reflection of the economic value it has created or lost. For example, in the case of lost sales, instead of focusing on accounting earnings, we focus on what we call "contributions," which are measured before taxes and before non-cash adjustments are made. Damages are usually calculated on a pretax basis because damages are taxable in most cases.

To understand the nature of "contribution," you need to understand two terms used in management accounting: *fixed costs* and *variable costs.* Almost every business has fixed and variable costs. Fixed costs are those that must be paid no matter what level of revenues is generated. These include rent on the business property, insurance, lighting and heating bills, interest on debts, wages to salaried employees, and so forth. A retail store selling stereos, television sets, and other consumer electronics equipment, for example, must meet each of the fixed costs just described, whether its sells one or one thousand stereo systems per week.

Variable costs, on the other hand, vary with the level of sales. Variable costs for the retailer described above include sales commissions, cost of goods sold, and shipping. For manufacturers, costs for electricity, materials, and direct labor generally vary with sales.

Exhibit 6-6 illustrates the relationship between fixed and variable costs for a business. Notice that fixed costs (FC) remain the same no matter what level of production or sales prevails. Once the fixed costs are given at a certain level, total costs increase by the amount of variable cost as the quantity increases. For example, at 1000 units, the variable costs are equal to the total cost less the fixed costs, T_1 - FC , and at 2000 units the variable costs increase to T_2 - FC. Thus, in the case of lost sales resulting from a contract violation, *the level of fixed costs does not affect the level of damages.* At 1000 units of production, total cost (T_1) increases above the fixed costs by the level of variable costs for that quantity; it increases further (to T_2) as production moves to 2000 units.

Exhibit 6-6. Fixed and Variable Costs

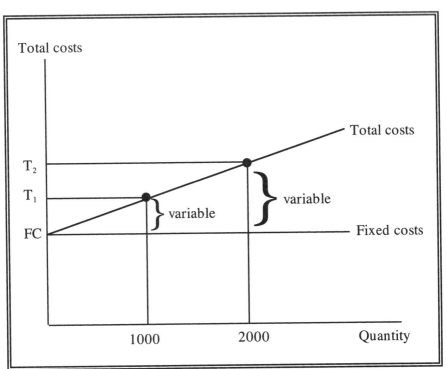

Contribution per unit is the price per unit minus the variable cost per unit. Similarly, in financial terms, total "contribution" is defined as *revenues less total variable cost.*

In determining damages to a business, it is often practical to assume that fixed costs remain the same and to use the concept of contribution. One such method to calculate damages follows these steps:

Step 1. Determine the revenues lost as a result of the damaging action – both since the action occurred and projected into the future.

Step 2. Subtract variable costs from the firm's revenues to determine the lost contribution.

Step 3. Determine an appropriate discount (or compounding) rate; in most cases, this will be the company's weighted average cost of capital;

Step 4. Use present value and future value calculations to bring historical and future losses to a single point in time.

BUSINESS DAMAGES EXAMPLE

Consider the case of Togs, a four store chain of women's specialty shops. The chain carried premium priced merchandise and had an exclusive contract with a Florida-based manufacturer to sell its "Vamp" designer line within a 30 mile radius of downtown Chicago. Togs bought more than 85% of its merchandise from this manufacturer. In addition to producing the product, the manufacturer compiled and distributed a catalog to the chain's customer base describing the nature and price of products carried by the chain. This catalog was printed under the Togs name.

Just prior to the second Christmas of the buying relationship, the management of Togs was shocked by the discovery that the manufacturer had been violating the terms of their agreement. It had been merchandising the "Vamp" line of women's clothing through a discount store competitor operating within the Togs' exclusive geographic area, and the clothing was being offered at a substantially lower price. Further, the manufacturer was mailing the same catalog – but under the discounter's logo and at reduced prices – to households throughout Togs' geographic area.

The impact of this contract violation on the four Togs stores was significant and felt almost immediately, with sales dropping dramatically. In determining the extent of the monetary damages to Togs, we follow these steps:

Step 1. Determine the revenues lost as a result of the damaging action. There are two categories of losses: historical losses – those revenues lost since the damaging action occurred; and future losses – those that are related to expected or potential future activities. We can better visualize these losses through Exhibit 6-7. As the directional arrows indicate, we will eventually need to adjust the dollar amounts of these losses, using time-value-of-money methods, to the date of the damage calculation.

Exhibit 6-7. Time Line of Damage Calculation for Togs

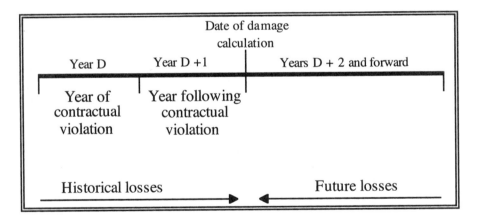

Historical losses. Let us begin with the first of these categories. One way of measuring the effects of the action of the errant manufacturer on Togs is to observe Togs' sales performance before and after the contract violation. As indicated by Exhibit 6-8, the chain, which was founded two years prior to this event, was experiencing sales growth at an annual rate of 4.74% in the year prior to the damage year (year D-1). During the year of the violation, Year D in our time line, business for Togs' four stores plummeted, dropping by 33%. The next year, Year D+1, was almost as bad, with an additional 31% decrease from the previous low mark. Because of the dramatic drop in actual sales at each of the four locations, all stores were closed at the end of Year D+2.

The retail clothing business has its ups and downs, and one might reasonably wonder if Togs' declining fortunes were not simply a reflection of an industry-wide downturn. To check this, we need to evaluate Togs' sales relative to the retail clothing industry in general.

Exhibit 6-8. Company vs. Industry: Sales Index

Year	Togs		Industry Average
	Annual Sales ($ millions)	% change from previous year	% change from previous year
D - 2	5.20	-	-
D - 1	5.45	4.74%	5.10%
D (year of damage)	3.65	-33.03%	4.40%
D + 1	2.52	-30.96%	**

**The industry average was not yet published at the time of damage calculation

Exhibit 6-8 indicates that industry sales growth slightly outpaced Togs' performance in the year just prior to the contract violation. In the year of the contract violation (Year D), industry sales grew by 4.4% while Togs' business was dropping by a third. Clearly, Togs' misfortune was not part of an industry-wide decline. Something else was going on, and Togs' management pointed to the effects of the contract violation.

Historical sales losses in this case are the difference between the sales Togs *would have achieved* in the absence of the contract violation and its *actual* sales. We can estimate the sales Togs would have achieved by increasing the sales it recorded for the year prior to the violation by the industry average growth rate of sales in the year the violation occurred. Thus, Year D-1 actual sales of $5.45 million are increased at the industry-wide rate of 4.4% to $5.69 million for Year D. Since industry data was not yet published for Year D+1 at the time we calculated the damages, we assume for simplicity's sake that Togs' sales would remain at $5.69 million.

With projected revenues now estimated, we need to determine the actual sales losses. They are calculated as the difference between what sales would have been and what they actually were, or:

> Projected sales in the absence of the contract violation *less* actual sales.

For Year D, the year in which the violation took place, this is:

> $5.69 million - $3.65 million = $2.04 million in lost sales

For the year following the violation, Year D+1, lost sales are:

> $5.69 million - $2.52 million = $3.17 million

This brings us to the date of the calculation and the end of historical sales losses. Losses beyond this point are future sales losses.

Future losses. One of the key issues in a damage calculation is the horizon over which projected damages are calculated. It is typically equal to the number of years over which earnings would have been generated in the absence of the illegal act and often considered a perpetuity into the future. The exact number of years varies from case to case. However, for the sake of illustration, we assume for simplicity that Togs' four stores close their doors at the end of D+1, the date of the damage calculation. During Year D+2, the company expects to incur expenses of $200,000 – all associated with prematurely ending its lease and other costs of closure.

Step 2. Adjust revenue losses by the variable costs and other costs to arrive at the lost contribution. In some situations, the firm's fixed costs are adjusted as a result of the damages and must be incorporated in the lost contribution calculation. We have now established revenue losses for Years D and D+1.

Revenue Losses	
Year D	Year D+1
$2.04 million	$3.17 million

These are lost revenues, but what is Togs' *lost contribution*? Obviously, Togs has variable costs associated with these revenues, and these must be subtracted to determine the contribution. Also, in some cases the damaged firm may have had to increase its advertising to compensate for the negative publicity associated with the illegal act. This increased advertising would be added to the damages. Similarly, if fixed costs were cut because of declining sales re-sulting from a patent violation, the reduction in fixed costs would be subtracted from the damage estimate. In other words, *an increase in expenses is typically added to the projected damages and a reduction in expenses is generally subtracted.* In this case, Togs' sales people are entirely on salary, so there are no commission expenses; in fact, the only variable cost associated with these sales is the *cost of goods sold.* As a result, Togs' lost contribution is computed simply as follows:

Lost contribution = Lost revenue - Cost of goods sold

Historically, Togs' cost of goods sold had been 60% of its sales. In other words, for every dollar in sales it generated, the store had spent 60 cents on the items sold, resulting in a 40 cent contribution – or 40% contribution margin. Knowing the contribution margin, we can compute the lost contribution:

Lost contribution = Lost revenue x Contribution margin

or, in this case:

Lost contribution = Lost revenue x 40%

So, for Year D through D+2, we can calculate Togs lost contribution and other expenses attributable to its closing as follows:

Year D	Year D+1	Year D+2
$2.04 million	$3.17 million	cost of closing
x 40%	x 40%	
$816,000	$1,268,000	$200,000

As with all financial dealings, these contribution losses and other costs need to be stated in current values. Since the damage calculation is being made as of the end of Year D+1, the Year D loss of $816,000 must be compounded for a period of one year. Likewise, the future loss of $200,000 must be discounted back to Year D+1. In both cases, an appropriate discount (or compounding) rate must be determined.

Step 3. Determine an appropriate discount rate. Financial experts accept the notion that when companies discount (or compound) their own cash flows, they need to do so at their own *cost of capital.* This was mentioned in the chapter on the time value of money, and developed more fully in the chapter devoted to the cost of capital.

For Togs, which had no debt, the cost of capital is based entirely on the cost of its shareholders' equity. Conveniently, the Capital Asset Pricing Model (CAPM) comes to our aid in determining Togs' cost of capital. Recall that the CAPM was used there to estimate the expected return on a security or portfolio of securities. It is this same return that Togs' shareholders "expect," given the riskiness of the company. The shareholders' expectation of return represents the cost to Togs of using their capital. Restated, the CAPM takes this form:

$$\text{Cost of Capital} = \text{Risk Free Rate} + \text{Beta x Market Premium}$$

Most of these variables are readily available from financial information service companies. The risk-free rate can be approximated using the rate on government securities, which for this case is found to be 7.6%. The market premium, which is the expected difference between the return on the market and the risk-free rate is approximated at 8%. Togs' beta is estimated as 1.5; this number is found by considering the values of similar public retailing firms. The cost of capital for Togs' shareholders, then, is calculated as:

$$\text{Cost of capital} = 7.6\% + 1.5 \times 8\%$$

$$= 19.6\%.$$

Step 4. Use present value and future value calculations to bring historical and future losses to a single point in time. We now have all the elements we need to calculate Togs' damages:

- losses and costs associated with the contract violation for each year;
- the discounting (compounding) rate; and
- the number of years, or periods, involved.

Exhibit 6-9 describes our plan for performing the calculations. As you can see, we want to put everything on the same time footing, namely, the end of Year D+1, the date of the damage calculation. The Year D+1 contribution loss is already expressed in these terms, so we have nothing to do there. The Year D contribution loss of $816 thousand, however, must be brought forward by finding its "future value." The $200 thousand business closing expense to be incurred in Year D+2 must be discounted back to Year D+1 by finding its "present value." (If any of these concepts are unfamiliar, refer to Chapter 2 on the time value of money).

Exhibit 6-9. Calculating Togs' Damages ($ thousands)

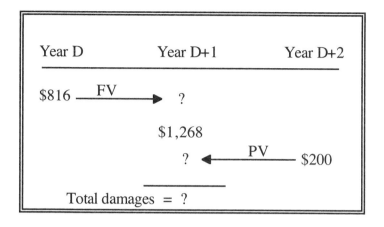

Using a financial calculator makes this job easy. For the Year D contribution loss:

PV = $816,000   n = 1   i = 19.6

Compute for FV. If you got $975,936, you would be exactly right.

Discounting the $200,000 closing expense back to Year D+1 is done as follows:

FV = $200,000   n = 1   i = 19.6%

Compute for PV. The answer is $167,224.

The total of these damages is indicated in Exhibit 6-10.

Exhibit 6-10. Total Togs Damages

Year D	Year D+1	Year D+2
$816,000 $\xrightarrow{\text{FV}}$ $975,936		
	1,268,000	
	167,224 $\xleftarrow{\text{PV}}$ $200,000	
Total damages =	$2,411,160	

To summarize, the following steps were used to determine the damages associated with Togs' lost earnings:

1. Analyze the historical track record of the firm and industry
2. Determine the historical lost sales
3. Determine the historical lost gross margin
4. Determine the historical lost contribution
5. Determine the projected lost sales
6. Determine the projected lost gross margin
7. Determine the projected lost contribution
8. Determine the cost of capital
9. Determine the compounded value of historical lost contribution
10. Determine the present value of projected lost contribution
11. Sum [9] and [10] to obtain the damage estimate

SECURITIES DAMAGE EXAMPLES

Damage claims frequently arise from securities cases. These can result from a number of causes including account churning, the recommendation of unsuitable securities by stockbrokers and investment advisors, and various forms of portfolio mismanagement. In addition, a broad range of cases result from disclosure issues.

Let us first consider the issue of portfolio mismanagement. There are many approaches to calculating damages from mismanagement. Three of the most common approaches are total portfolio loss, market-adjusted portfolio loss, and risk-adjusted portfolio loss.

Total portfolio loss. The most basic approach is to simply determine the total loss in the portfolio's value. Consider, for example, a portfolio having an initial value of $10 million. The portfolio's value fell by 80% to $2 million; thus, the resulting damage claim is $8 million.

Market-adjusted portfolio loss. The total portfolio loss approach is easy to figure, but it ignores the movement of the market. If the market fell by 20% during the same period, and assuming the portfolio is broadly diversified, one might argue that a quarter of the portfolio's losses are attributable to the general decline of the market, with other losses potentially being attributable to mismanagement.

Risk-adjusted portfolio loss. In many cases, even the market-adjusted approach fails to represent the appropriate damages. This is because it does not recognize the inherent volatility of the particular portfolio, which is not necessarily a close match to the overall market.

Consider, for example, a portfolio structured – at the client's direction – to be 20% more volatile than the overall market. (This client expected the market to rise). Recalling our discussion of "betas" in the chapter on securities, this portfolio should have a beta of 1.2. It would then be expected to outpace a rising market by 20%, or fall 20% further than a falling market. If, however, the market dropped by 10% and the portfolio dropped by 80%, part of the portfolio's losses would be explained by the market's decline while another might represent mismanagement.

Consider our $10 million portfolio whose beta equals 1.2. The risk free rate during the damage horizon was 6.5% and the S&P Total Return Index fell 10.0%. The expected return on the portfolio was:

$$= 6.5\% + 1.2\ (\ -10.0\% - 6.5\%)$$
$$= -13.3\%$$

Thus, the portfolio would have been expected to fall to $8.67 million ($10 million less $1.333 million). But in reality it fell 80% to $2 million. An expert analyzing the mismanagement would evaluate the unexplained $6.67 million loss.

NON-DISCLOSURE DAMAGES

Two of the approaches frequently used to determine damages in disclosure litigation will be briefly mentioned. One approach assesses the price drop of the firm's shares and multiplies the drop in price by the number of outstanding shares. Thus, if the stock dropped by $4 per share as a result of a particular material factor not disclosed or erroneously disclosed to the market, the damages would be $4 per share times the 2 million shares outstanding, or $8 million. Under this approach, those owning the stock would receive a damage award even though they would have experienced the drop were the information appropriately revealed. In the second approach, the specific number of shares which were damaged is determined. Using this technique, one determines the number of shares which were bought following the erroneous disclosure and held until proper disclosure was made. The calculations performed in this manner are known as "fraud on the market" calculations. Such fraud on the market models are often complex and require data and assumptions about the trading pattern of the security. This topic is discussed more thoroughly in Chapter 3.

Chapter 7
Bankruptcy And Fraudulent Conveyances

This chapter examines issues of financial distress that afflict business entities. The term financial distress covers a wide spectrum of financial difficulties. These difficulties range from a high degree of uncertainty over future profitability and cash flow to a firm's inability to meet its current obligations. The last half of the chapter extends issues of financial distress to a particular area of litigation: cases of fraudulent conveyance involving leveraged buyouts and other recapitalizations.

A firm's severe financial distress is typically reflected in a situation where its cash inflows are insufficient to cover its cash outflows including payments to its capital providers. Such a firm may continue operating, while generating below market rates of return. As long as investors are willing to continue supplying the firm with capital, or accept an inferior return, such a firm can remain in business. In some cases, lenders who see the firm's problems as transitory may provide additional funds or accept "interest only" payments on current obligations. Equity investors may contribute more capital or accept a temporary cut in dividends. Financial distress by itself does not necessarily imply any immediate consequences. For example, during one of the worst auto recessions in recent memory, Ford Motor Company was hemorrhaging red ink. Its fixed obligations for interest payments and overhead exceeded its cash inflows by a wide margin. Ford initially managed to meet its obligations by supplementing cash inflows with a reduction in its cash reserves. Eventually, for the first time in a generation, it discontinued paying cash dividends to its common shareholders. Investors continued to hold Ford shares, however, because they could see beyond the period of distress to a brighter future for the company. In fact, Ford Motor Company rebounded from its distress, and within a decade was reporting profits beyond all expectations.

Financial distress, like that encountered in the Ford example, typically results in corrective action by the firm itself. It attempts to stem any cash insufficiency and may take any one of a number of actions, including:

- Dividend reductions
- Layoffs
- Hiring freezes
- Capital expenditure and R&D cutbacks
- Debt reduction through exchange offers (debt for equity)
- Plant closings
- Asset sales
- Renegotiation with creditors

CAUSES OF DISTRESS

While there are numerous causes of financial distress, the three most frequently cited reasons are: mismanagement, debt overload, and economic activity.

Mismanagement comes in many forms. Frequently, a successful firm expands too rapidly, creating commitments it cannot meet or overhead that future levels of business cannot support. Sometimes, management is inappropriate for the business at hand. The founder/CEO of a growing high-tech company may be a wizard in the research lab, but a complete zero when it comes to decision-making and the day-to-day business of managing employees. In other cases, key executive roles are filled by people unsuited by experience or temperament for their positions: a trucking executive running a major department store; a takeover specialist at the controls of a major airline. The failure to renew the company's product line, the growth of staff bureaucracies, and misallocation of capital investments are some other reasons that financial distress occurs – and each can be laid at the feet of management.

Debt overload has become a dominant cause of financial distress and has resulted in large corporate failures. Continental Airlines, Allied Stores/Federated Department Stores, and Southland Corporation were typical of firms undone by debt financing. While many leveraged buyouts were appropriately capitalized, debt was excessive in others. For example, in the case of Morse Tool, a division of the former Gulf and Western, the debt-equity ratio resulting from its leveraged buyout was 150-to-1. In other cases, the debt load was either egregious or great enough to cause firms to enter a period of financial distress. For example, Mr. Giancarlo Paretti bought the billion dollar MGM Studio using only $89,000 of his own equity capital. The rest was borrowed.

The third major cause of financial distress is the economy. During a recession, many industries are devastated by a decline in demand. Airlines, companies in the leisure industry, producers of consumer durables, and numerous others are significantly affected by lost sales. Those firms with large debt levels are doubly impacted by a recession. For example, America West cited the recessionary environment, high debt service costs and its resulting cash flow difficulties in its bankruptcy filing.

INFORMAL REORGANIZATION

Firms in financial distress must determine if their problems are short-term and the firm is viable or whether the firm's difficulties represent a permanent economic problem with the firm's viability in doubt. In assessing the firm's alternative courses of action, it must determine whether a voluntary settlement should be attempted through an informal process of negotiation or whether formal bankruptcy is more appropriate.

Voluntary settlements, often called *workouts*, are driven by the economics of the bankruptcy process. When a firm experiences financial distress, both creditors and debtors can usually benefit if they can avoid the formal bankruptcy process. Creditors are able to receive a greater fraction of their outstanding claims by avoiding the sometimes significant costs associated with formal bankruptcy. Debtors are able to continue operating the firm without the stigma of formal bankruptcy. Furthermore, the owners are able to maximize the chance of recovering any funds for themselves.

Typically, the debtor calls a meeting of its creditors. The creditors then appoint a committee consisting of the largest creditors and possibly several small creditors. If the committee determines that restructuring is feasible, the recommendations of the creditors are then formulated in a preliminary reorganization plan.

Restructuring may call for the owners of the distressed firm to inject new equity capital – either out of their own pockets or from other investors. It may result in a recommendation that unproductive assets or underperforming lines of business be sold. In any case, the plan of the creditor committee is discussed and negotiated with the debtor before a final agreement is reached. If the committee determines that the firm should be liquidated rather than reorganized, a liquidation plan is drawn up.

If it is determined that the firm can be informally reorganized, that is, without the formal process of Chapter 11, two frequently used tools are employed to sustain the organization. These tools are *extension* and *composition*.

Extension provides creditors with the full amount of the funds owed to them, but allows the debtor additional time to meet its obligations. For example, consider a distressed company with $20 million of debt that has been paying interest and is scheduled by the loan agreement to repay the principal amount next year. In its current situation, it is already clear that it will be unable to come up with the $20 million. The creditor agrees to an extension of two years for the principal repayment. Interest payments will, however, continue.

Composition reduces the payments received by the creditor. It is essentially a pro rata cash settlement of creditor claims. Specifically, creditors receive only a partial payment, where it is agreed that a uniform percentage of each dollar owed is paid to satisfy the creditors' claims. For example, a creditor may agree to make modifications to the credit agreements such that there is either a reduction in principal, reduction in interest, substitution of equity for debt, or some combination of these approaches.

What is the cost of an extension or composition arrangement? If you are representing the creditor in an extension or composition arrangement, how much of a hit is your client taking by extending the payment time line or reducing the borrower's obligations for principal or interest repayments? You can use the lessons of time value of money to good effect here.

Examples. The debtor is paying $100 thousand per year in interest, with the entire principal amount of $800 thousand due two years hence. Because of the debtor's distress, your client, the lender, says, "I'll give you a break. I'll extend the due date on the principal and interest for a full year."

To determine the value of this extension to your client, you find the difference between the present value of the cash flows (interest and repayment of principal) under the old arrangement and the new one. As illustrated by the "OLD" panel of Exhibit 7-1, at a 12.5% discount rate, the value of the pre-extension payment stream is $800,000. Increased risk has caused the discount rate in the "NEW" panel to be 18%. At 18%, the value of the post-extension cash flows is $632,500. The difference between the present value of the two sets of cash flows, $167,500, represents the cost of the extension.

Exhibit 7-1. Determining the Cost of an Extension

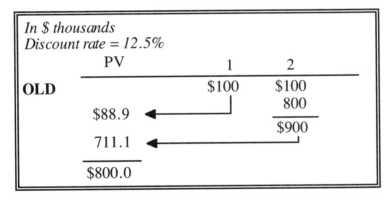

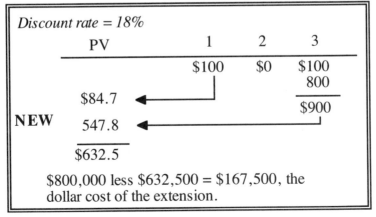

Now consider another situation involving a composition arrangement in which your client, a creditor, has agreed to reduce a distressed firm's annual payment (representing interest and principal) from $200,000 to $150,000 per year. The loan has another four years to run. You can find the present value of your client's generosity by simply finding the present value of four future sums, each of $50,000. As indicated by Exhibit 7-2 and using the client's cost of capital of 15% as the discount rate, your client is giving up $142,750 through this composition agreement.

Exhibit 7-2. Determining the Cost of a Composition

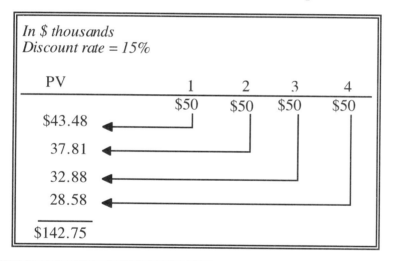

Note: Your financial calculator provides a big short-cut when you have situations like this last one, in which 1) the cash flows are same, and 2) they occur in a sequence of periods. Simply enter the amount of the cash flow (50) as PMT, enter the discount rate (15) as i, enter the number of periods (4) as n. Now calculate for PV. This saves you the trouble of calculating the present value of each cash flow and summing them up.

In some cases, a third approach is used in a voluntary settlement, *creditor control*. The creditor committee may determine that it is not in the creditor's best interest to have the debtor management continue to operate the business. As a result, they may replace the operating management to increase the likelihood that all of the outstanding claims will be settled. Such a replacement of management may be used in conjunction with an extension or composition.

INFORMAL LIQUIDATION

If, after the firm has been investigated by the creditor committee, it is determined that a liquidation of assets will yield the greatest return for creditors, an informal liquidation may take place. The avoidance of formal bankruptcy and liquidation procedures can result in higher and quicker payments to the firm's creditors. The difficulty in instituting an informal liquidation is that all creditors must agree to the terms of the settlement. Because of the complexities and conflicts among different creditor classes in larger organizations, such a process is usually only implemented in small firms.

An informal liquidation is often achieved through an *assignment*. In an assignment, the debtor's assets are transferred to a third party with responsibility to liquidate the assets. The third party is referred to as the assignee. It then distributes the funds to the creditors, and if any remains, to the firm's shareholders. Since the assignment process is quicker than a formal liquidation, creditors are often able to sell inventory before it becomes obsolete and collect a higher percentage of outstanding receivables.

BANKRUPTCY

Formal bankruptcy in the United States differs significantly from bankruptcy laws in most other countries. In the United States, the laws provide an opportunity for the debtor to reorganize, often with the debtor maintaining control of the enterprise. In many other countries, a debtor's property is auctioned off if it cannot pay its debts. The core of the bankruptcy legislation is the Bankruptcy Code.

The two most relevant provisions for corporate bankruptcy are Chapter 7 and Chapter 11 of the Bankruptcy Code. Chapter 7 describes the procedures to be used in liquidating a business. Such liquidations typically result when a fair and equitable basis for the firm's reorganization does not exist. Chapter 11 describes the procedures for reorganizing a failed firm. It does not distinguish between voluntary and involuntary reorganizations. If a feasible basis does not exist for reorganizing the company, liquidation of the firm's assets will take place. Interestingly, a reorganization in Chapter 11 frequently involves a "liquidation" of all of the estate's assets. Liquidations by the firm through a Chapter 11 often yield a greater price than trustee conducted liquidations of firms in Chapter 7.

CHAPTER 11 REORGANIZATION

A reorganization petition under Chapter 11 is filed with the court. A Chapter 11 reorganization may be either voluntary or involuntary. An involuntary reorganization is typically initiated by three or more unpaid creditors, while a voluntary reorganization is initiated by the debtor itself. If it is an involuntary petition and challenged by the debtor, the court must determine whether the firm is insolvent.

Five steps must be taken in initiating and executing a Chapter 11 reorganization: filing, appointment of a debtor-in-possession (DIP) or trustee, submission and consideration of the reorganization plan, acceptance of the reorganization plan, and the payment of expenses.

Benefits to the firm. One of the major benefits of any bankruptcy filing is the *automatic stay.* The stay immediately halts most litigation and collection activities against the firm. It is not uncommon for debtors to file for bankruptcy in anticipation of foreclosure to prevent the loss of key assets or to prevent litigation or collection activities. While the stay is not permanent, it provides the debtor with time to focus on the affairs of the firm and to improve its cash flow. Another benefit of a Chapter 11 filing is the possible delay of interest and principal payments.

The debtor firm, upon filing of the reorganization petition, becomes a debtor-in-possession (DIP). As a DIP, the firm has important new opportunities to obtain loans, making it possible to continue operations and meet working capital needs. Normally, a failed firm would find few, if any, individuals or organizations willing to lend it money. As a DIP, however, loans are easier to acquire for the simple reason that loans to DIPs become senior to all other unsecured debt. If not for this provision, lenders would be reluctant to advance any funds to a DIP.

These provisions break the vicious circle that typically afflicts the financially distressed firm. In that cycle, suppliers observe that the firm is falling behind in its payments and either reduce or eliminate credit terms to it. Lenders, too, note the firm's difficult situation and withhold credit. Lacking supplies and working capital, the firm's situation begins a downward spiral. Upon the filing of bankruptcy, however, these suppliers and lenders may again be willing to provide credit, knowing that their claims, classified as "administrative expenses," virtually always receive priority over other unsecured claims. In many cases, this new ability to secure credit breaks the momentum toward a failure for the distressed firm.

The debtor-in-possession has several key responsibilities. One of the first is to value the firm as a going concern and to assess its liquidation value. If the liquidation value is greater, liquidation is recommended. If the going concern value is greater, the DIP will recommend reorganization, in which case the DIP must submit a plan of reorganization to the court.

The DIP is given the exclusive right for 120 days after filing for bankruptcy to submit such a reorganization plan. It is then given 60 days to obtain an agreement from each of the parties. The court, however, may extend either of these dates.

During the reorganization, corporate management is given wide latitude in exercising its business judgment. Operational decisions will usually be made with little interference from the court. However, a major change takes place in the governance of the organization. The officers and directors must shift their attention from protecting the interests of the firm's shareholders to protecting the interests of the firm's creditors. Decisions regarding salaries and benefits, which may have been appropriate prior to the Chapter 11 filing, may now be inappropriate. This is of particular concern in the case of a closely held firm, in which managers and directors may be reluctant to institute required cuts in both staffing and compensation.

The costs of Chapter 11. While the benefits of a Chapter 11 filing for the debtor are significant, the costs may also be sizable. In addition to the intangible costs associated with the shift in allegiance of the officers and directors to creditors, there are sizable tangible costs, such as the transaction costs associated with the filing. Innumerable hours are spent by accountants and lawyers fending off requests by creditors and obtaining court approval for certain activities resulting in major cash outlays. Moreover, the decision-making process is often slowed. Management operates in a "fishbowl," its decisions and uses of financial resources scrutinized by creditors who, in some cases, attempt to remove management and appoint a trustee to run the business. In other cases, they press to convert the Chapter 11 filing to a Chapter 7 liquidation.

DIP management also operates with the stigma of bankruptcy, which, in itself, may make Chapter 7 more likely. How many customers, after all, want to do business with a firm that may not be in business a year from now? How many manufacturers want to sign an agreement with a parts supplier that may evaporate, leaving them without parts and without a reliable supplier? Moreover, competitors will frequently use the Chapter 11 filing to bad mouth the firm to its customers.

The feasibility issue. A major issue surrounding the reorganization plan is its feasibility. Usually, the proposed capital structure plays a significant role in the determination of whether the plan is feasible and workable. Because of the fixed nature of the interest and principal payments, these fixed charges are usually modified in the recapitalization. Often, under the recapitalization, debt is exchanged for equity, maturities are lengthened, or interest rates are reduced. The revised capital structure must be able to support the firm's projected operations. Sometimes, to assure the feasibility of the proposed plan and to remain a going concern, the DIP will plan to simultaneously cut costs and modernize key equipment to reduce the cost of goods sold. It may include marketing or operational changes in its plan. It may also recommend focusing on certain products and territories or it may include a plan to sell assets or divisions.

The order of claims. In addition to feasibility, the reorganization plan must be fair and equitable to the various claimants. Those claims with the highest legal priority must be satisfied prior to those with lower priority. This is accomplished by having senior claimants receive distribution rights in the reorganized firm at least equal to that which they held prior to bankruptcy. Claimants may receive different securities in the restructured firm than those they previously owned. For example, a senior bondholder may find himself receiving a combination of newly issued debt securities, preferred stock, and common stock.

Court approval of reorganization. Once approved by the court, the plan is voted on by the firm's creditors and equity holders. The creditors are separated into classes with similar claims. A reorganization plan is considered accepted by a class of creditors if creditors representing two-thirds of the amount of debt and more than one-half of the number of creditors agree to the plan. Moreover, two-thirds of the amount of each equity group must also approve the reorganization plan for it to be accepted. If a plan is not voted for by all the creditors, each class must receive at least as much as they would have received under Chapter 7. The court may confirm the plan in spite of the dissent of a particular class. When the court mandates such a plan that has not been agreed to by all classes, it is termed a *"cramdown."*

After the plan is either approved or disapproved, expenses incurred in the process are presented to the court for approval and, if accepted, are paid within a reasonable period of time.

Reorganization Illustration: An overly ambitious expansion plan caused Legal Computer Systems to experience severe cash shortages. Unable to meet payroll and significantly behind in its debt obligations, it filed for Chapter 11. The firm's value as a going concern is estimated as $5,000,000. The claims on the firm's assets are listed as:

Secured Debt	$2,500,000
Unsecured Claims:	
Notes payable	1,000,000
Subordinated debentures	3,500,000
(subordinated to notes payable)	
Other general creditors	3,000,000
Total Unsecured Claims	7,500,000
Total Claims	$10,000,000

Given that the firm's value as a going concern is estimated as $5,000,000, and it has secured debt of $2,500,000, the following relationship is derived:

$$\frac{\text{The value available}}{\text{for unsecured claimants}} = \frac{\text{Total}}{\text{Value}} - \frac{\text{Secured}}{\text{Debt}}$$
$$= 5,000,000 - 2,500,000$$
$$= \$2,500,000$$

Furthermore, given that the value available for unsecured claims is $2,500,000, and the total amount of the firm's unsecured claims is $7,500,000, a key figure to be used in the reorganization plan is:

$$\frac{\text{Value available for unsecured claims}}{\text{Total unsecured claims}} = \frac{2,500,000}{7,500,000} = 33\%$$

Based on this information, the reorganization plan can be developed as follows:

> *Secured debt*: Their original claim was $2,500,000. They will receive $2,500,000 of mortgage bonds.
> *Notes payable*: Their original claim was $1,000,000. Given that 33% of $1,000,000 is only $333,333, the additional $666,667 will be taken from the class of subordinated debentures to satisfy the class of notes payable (total: $333,333 + $666,667 = $1 million).
> *Subordinated debentures*: Their original claim was $3,500,000. Given that 33% of this amount is $1,166,667 and $666,667 was transferred to satisfy the holders of notes payable, this groups claim after subordination is $500,000 ($1,166,667 - $666,667 = $500,000).
> *Other general creditors*: Given that the total value available to unsecured claimants is $2,500,000, the remaining value for the other general creditors after accounting for both notes payable and subordinated debentures will be $1,000,000 ($2,500,000 - $1,000,000 - $500,000 = $1,000,000).

The reorganization plan can be summarized as follows:

Original Security	Pre-bankruptcy Claim (A)	Post-bankruptcy Claim (B)	B÷A	Form of New Claim
Secured debt	2,500,000	2,500,000	100%	Mortgage bonds
Notes payable	1,000,000	1,000,000	100%	Debentures
Subordinated deb.	3,500,000	500,000	14%	Preferred stock
Other general creditors	3,000,000	1,000,000	33%	Common stock

CHAPTER 7 LIQUIDATION

When a firm is worth more dead than alive, when reorganization is not feasible, and when the firm's creditors are likely to run a greater risk of loss if it continues to operate, the firm enters Chapter 7. As a practical matter, firms often liquidate in Chapter 11 rather than convert to Chapter 7. A judge typically appoints a trustee to oversee the liquidation and protect the creditors' interests. The trustee has responsibility for all aspects of the liquidation, including record keeping, cash disbursement, and all reports to the court on the progress of the liquidation.

If assets are distributed in a liquidation under Chapter 7, the following represents the priority of claims:

1. Administration expenses associated with the bankruptcy proceedings.
2. Expenses incurred following the bankruptcy filing, but prior to the appointment of a trustee. (This step occurs only in an involuntary bankruptcy.)
3. Unpaid wages (subject to a certain limit per person) earned within the three months prior to the bankruptcy filing.
4. Unpaid employee benefit plan contributions which should have been paid within six months prior to the bankruptcy filing. (These claims plus wages may not exceed a maximum allowable amount per person.)
5. Unsecured customer deposits (subject to a certain limit per person).
6. Taxes due to the federal, state, or county government and any other governmental agency.
7. Secured creditors, who are entitled to receive the proceeds of the sale of specific property, regardless of the above priorities.
8. General, or unsecured, creditors, including the unsatisfied portion of secured loans.
9. Preferred stockholders, who can receive up to the par value of their preferred stock.

10. Common stockholders, who will receive the remaining funds.

Liquidation Illustration: A & A Container, a rapidly growing firm specializing in the manufacture of paperboard containers, has a balance sheet presented in Exhibit 7-3. Because of a recent change in technology, a number of new competitors have entered the field and have captured a large segment of the market with their high quality and low cost. As a result, the firm entered Chapter 7, with a bankruptcy trustee liquidating the firm's assets. The trustee was able to obtain $4.1 million for the firm's current assets and $2.9 million for its fixed assets. Thus the $10.55 million of A & A liabilities ($4.95 million short-term and $5.6 million long-term) exceeded the $7.0 million market value of its assets.

Exhibit 7-4 illustrates the distribution of the $7.0 million of proceeds to various claimants. The expenses incurred in administering the bankruptcy and the liability associated with satisfying the unpaid bills in the time period between the bankruptcy filing and the appointment of the trustee totaled $450,000.

In addition, based on the priority of claims, accrued wages, unpaid employee benefits and taxes payable at A & A Container are distributed prior to any distribution to unsecured creditors. Furthermore, proceeds from the sale of assets serving as collateral for secured obligations are also distributed to secured creditors prior to any payment to the firm's general creditors. As illustrated in Exhibit 7-4, the trustee, after making these payments, has $2,000,000 available for payment to the unsecured creditors. Since the amount claimed by the unsecured creditors is $6,000,000, the pro rata distribution is $.33 for each $1.00 claimed (see Exhibit 7-5).

Exhibit 7-3. A & A Container Balance Sheet

Assets		Liabilities + Equity	
Cash	$21,000	Accounts payable	$2,300,000
Marketable securities	30,000	Notes payable	1,000,000
Accounts receivable	2,160,000	Accrued wages[1]	885,000
Inventories	3,840,000	Unpaid employee	175,000
Prepaid expenses	6,000	benefits[2]	
Total current assets	6,057,000	Taxes payable	590,000
Land	1,450,000	Total current liabilities	4,950,000
Net plant & equipment	4,990,000	Mortgage bonds[3]	2,900,000
Total fixed assets	6,440,000	Debentures	2,700,000
Total	$12,497,000	Total long-term debt	5,600,000
		Common stock (50,000 shares, $1 par)	800,000
		Paid-in capital in excess of par	750,000
		Retained earnings	397,000
		Total stockholders' equity	1,947,000
		Total	$12,497,000

Exhibit 7-4. Distribution of Proceeds from A & A Container Liquidation

Cash received from liquidation	$7,000,000
- Administration expenses and unpaid interim bills	450,000
- Wages owed to employees	885,000
- Unpaid employee benefits	175,000
- Taxes owed	590,000
=Cash available for distribution to creditors	4,900,000
- Mortgage bonds secured by tangible fixed assets	2,900,000
=Cash available for unsecured creditors	$2,000,000

---

[1] These wages were earned within 3 months prior to the bankruptcy filing.
[2] These unpaid benefit contributions were due within the six months prior to the bankruptcy filing.
[3] These mortgage bonds are secured by all the firm's tangible fixed assets.

Exhibit 7-5. Distribution to Unsecured Creditors

Type of Unsecured Creditor	Amount of Claim	Received from Liquidation at 33%
Accounts payable	$2,300,000	$766,667
Notes payable	1,000,000	333,333
Debentures	2,700,000	900,000
Total	$6,000,000	$2,000,000

PREPACKAGED BANKRUPTCIES

Because of the cost and time associated with formal Chapter 11 proceedings, a number of firms have chosen to use a type of reorganization which combines the benefits of an informal workout with that of a formal Chapter 11 reorganization.

Like in a workout, the debtor negotiates the terms of the restructuring with each of the firm's creditors. This is accomplished prior to the firm's formal bankruptcy filing. Simultaneously with the filing or shortly thereafter, a reorganization plan is also filed with the court. By obtaining the approvals prior to filing the petition, the debtor is frequently able to have its plan confirmed by the court soon after the filing. Significant prepackaged bankruptcies include Southland, Republic Health, Resorts International, and Kash N' Karry Food Stores.

FRAUDULENT CONVEYANCES AND LBOs

A leveraged buyout transaction may result in a fraudulent conveyance if the action of setting up the LBO left the firm insolvent or with an unreasonably small capital base.[1] The firm's unsecured creditors may claim that they were in a passive position at the time of the buyout, unable to protect their interests and, as a result, those interests were prejudiced by the added security interest given to secured lenders with no equivalent payment in return. Should the firm fail subsequent to the LBO, its unsecured creditors may argue that appropriate financial analysis at the time of the buyout should have revealed that the firm would be unable to tolerate the added debt burden associated with the deal.

Many bankrupt leveraged buyouts, including Morse Tool, Revco, Wieboldt Stores and others have been litigated under the sixteenth-century English common law concept of fraudulent conveyance. Bankruptcy trustees have used this concept in seeking to recover funds, and junk bond holders have also used it to seek remedies for their losses.

Fraudulent conveyance liability is one of the major risks facing participants when an LBO fails. If the court determines that a fraudulent conveyance has occurred, senior lenders may lose their seniority by having their liens and security set aside. Selling shareholders may be required to return the proceeds of the sale, and advisers to the transaction may be required to return fees received. Furthermore, the board of directors of the selling company may be found liable for significant damages. As a result, the selling company's board, advisers, lenders and significant selling shareholders are thrust into the position of having to justify the financial and legal aspects of the sale.

To determine whether a fraudulent conveyance has occurred in an LBO, first the court must determine whether

---

[1] The following discussion is based extensively on the publication, "Fraudulent Conveyance In Leveraged Buyouts: The Financial Issues," co-authored by A. Michel and I. Shaked, and published by Cornerstone Research.

"reasonable equivalent value" or "fair consideration" was transferred in the transaction. The lack of fair consideration is necessary – but not sufficient – to prove a fraudulent conveyance. Second, it must be proven that at the time of the LBO or recapitalization, the firm was either insolvent or left with an unreasonably small amount of capital as a result of the transaction – so small, in fact, that the firm had poor prospects for survival. Much of the financial analysis surrounding fraudulent conveyance litigation addresses this second issue.

Assessing fair consideration. With regard to fair consideration, the Court must determine whether the firm received sufficient value for taking on new obligations in the LBO. Typically, the bank lending funds for an LBO requires collateral, either in the form of current assets, such as inventory or accounts receivable, or fixed assets such as plant and equipment. In return, the bank lends the firm funds that are used to pay the selling shareholders. While these funds sometimes go through the company and then to the selling shareholders, they often are channeled directly from the bank to the selling shareholders. In either case, the firm never actually has use of the funds; it merely acts as a conduit. Exhibit 7-6 shows these flows of funds in various structures of LBO transactions.

Once it has been established that the firm did not receive fair value in exchange for the security interest in its assets, the unsecured creditors typically retain a financial expert in an attempt to prove either insolvency or undercapitalization.

Assessing solvency. The definition of solvency for purposes of fraudulent conveyance litigation differs significantly from standard Generally Accepted Accounting Principles (GAAP). Under the Uniform Fraudulent Conveyance Act and its successor, the Uniform Fraudulent Transfer

Exhibit 7-6. Examples of LBO Transaction Structures

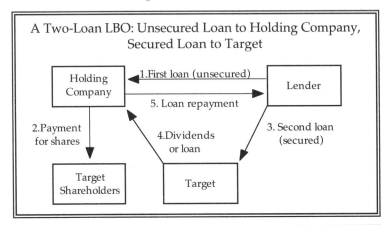

A Two-Loan LBO: Unsecured Loan to Holding Company,
Secured Loan to Target

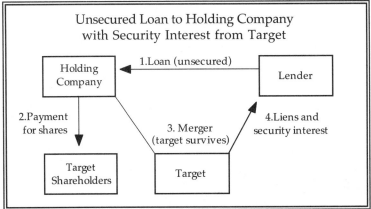

Unsecured Loan to Holding Company
with Security Interest from Target

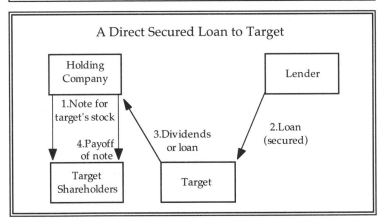

A Direct Secured Loan to Target

(Continued on next page)

Exhibit 7-6. (Continued). Examples of LBO Transaction
            Structures

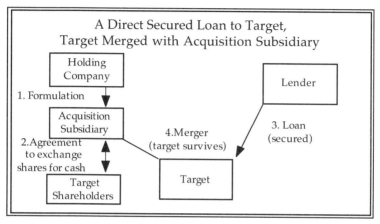

Source: Allen Michel and Israel Shaked, "The LBO Nightmare:
Fraudulent Conveyance Risk," *Financial Analysts Journal,* March-
April 1990, pp. 43-44.

Act, a firm can be considered insolvent when the fair value
of its assets in a reasonably prompt sale is less than the
amount that will be required to pay its probable liability
on existing debts. All debts are considered, whether mature or not mature, liquidated or unliquidated, absolute,
fixed or contingent.

Under this definition, off-balance sheet liabilities
such as health benefits and unfunded pension liabilities
are typically included in the analysis of the firm's financial
condition. The analysis also must take into account any
other contingent liabilities and all other liabilities potentially affecting solvency. Thus, in some cases the liabilities
included in a fraudulent conveyance analysis may be substantially greater than those represented on the books of
the corporation. In other cases, however, certain liabilities

on the firm's books may not represent claims that must be paid. For example, under the assumption that the firm was a going concern at the time of the LBO transaction, the tax liability on the firm's books may not represent an actual claim by the IRS. This occurs when net operating loss carryforwards would have offset any tax liability generated either through a brief period of profitability or through the sale of assets.

Analysis of the asset side of the balance sheet also differs from traditional GAAP analysis. The value of the firm's assets is not their traditional book value, but rather their "fair salable value." To obtain that fair salable value, one typically adjusts the book value of the assets upward or downward to reflect market conditions. Whether going concern or liquidation value should be used must also be determined. Generally, courts have considered the going concern value appropriate unless the firm is deemed to be on its deathbed, often referred to as "close to shutting its doors."

A firm is on its deathbed if it can be shown that it has little chance of survival in the near term. Yet prior losses – even extended losses – do not necessarily place a firm on its deathbed. Other evidence usually is necessary to substantiate that the firm is on its deathbed. This may include a combination of one or more factors, such as: lack of available collateral and borrowing power, newly surfaced competition, technological change, serious union obstacles to planned change, loss of key personnel prior to the transaction, major image deterioration, new management with a lack of industry experience, non-competitive cost structure, and others. Without strong substantiation that the firm is on its deathbed, however, the going concern assumption will usually be appropriate.

Going concern value and deathbed value may differ substantially. In fact, a key battle between plaintiff and defendant concerning valuation often centers on whether going concern or liquidation value is more appropriate. The confrontation is particularly intense when the company files Chapter 11 soon after the transaction. In such circumstances, the trustee may argue that the firm was insolvent at the time of the deal because of the leverage taken on to effect the transaction. However, the fact that a firm filed Chapter 11 soon after a buyout may well be irrelevant in determining whether it was insolvent at the time of the transaction, particularly if it can be shown that intervening events contributed to its bankruptcy. The courts in recent cases have considered solvency at the time of the transaction – not whether the firm became insolvent at some later time.

Fortunately, several methods of financial analysis can be used to determine the issue of solvency. These include an analysis of a fair value balance sheet, the use of multiples derived from the firm's industry group, and discounted cash flow analysis (DCF). To help you understand these methods, we apply them to a company we have studied earlier in this book, an interstate transportation company called Great Lakes Bus Lines, whose post-LBO balance sheet information is presented in Exhibit 7-7.

1. *Fair value balance sheet approach.* This approach to assessing insolvency restates the company's balance sheet to reflect true market values. As indicated by Exhibit 7-7, we have made a number of adjustments to the balance sheet on the asset side. The company's current assets were found to be sound, but its long-term assets needed adjustments. We have canceled out Net Property, Plant & Equipment since this represents historical values less de-

preciation taken on the basis of GAAP rule and not the rules of the marketplace. In its place, under "additions," we have substituted an appraised estimate of the fair value of the company's assets – what it could get for them in a fairly rapid liquidation.

The book values of "Other Assets" have been deleted. In a liquidation, you cannot take these book values to the bank. However, $5.91 has been added to "Other Assets," better reflecting market value. The liabilities were restated, resulting in an equity value equal to the firm's restated assets ($103.37 million) less its liabilities ($90.89 million), or $12.48 million.

2. *The market multiple approach.* This method of analysis begins with the notion that we can estimate the fair value of a company's assets by determining what the market has demonstrated as its willingness to pay for the assets of similar companies in the same industry. This method is particularly useful when the company we are concerned with is a privately held company in a universe of similar companies that are publicly held and traded. We can find, for example, a number of competing companies whose share prices are available, or whose corporate values have been recently established through sale or merger. Using these as proxies, we can, with appropriate adjustments, find the value of another company's assets. This approach has already been discussed in our chapter on valuation. But we will go through the exercise again here to determine the solvency of Great Lakes Bus Lines.

No two companies in the same industry are likely to have the same level of assets. So how can we compare two companies? One way is to compare a measure of value such as the Business Enterprise Value with a measure of the firm's operations. Let's start by considering multiples

Exhibit 7-7. Great Lakes Bus Lines Fair Value Balance Sheet ($ millions)

	BOOK VALUE	Adjustments		FAIR VALUE
		Deletions	Additions	
	(1)	- (2)	+ (3)	= (4)
Current Assets:				
Accounts Receivable	$ 24.49			$ 24.49
Inventories	1.45			1.45
Prepaid Expenses	2.92			2.92
Total Current Assets	28.86			**28.86**
Fixed Assets:				
Property, Plant & Equipment	66.82	(66.82)	68.60	68.60
Less: Accumulated Depreciation	(11.81)	11.81		
Net Property, Plant & Equipment	55.01	(55.01)	68.60	**68.60**
Other Assets:				
Operating Rights	3.42	(3.42)	3.00	3.00
Deferred Financing and Software Costs	4.64	(4.64)		
Prepaid Pension, Deposits, Other	3.49	(3.49)	2.91	2.91
Total Other Assets	11.55	(11.55)	5.91	**5.91**
Total Assets	$ 95.42	$(66.56)	$ 74.51	**$103.37**

(Continued on next page)

Exhibit 7-7. (Continued)

	BOOK VALUE	Adjustments		FAIR VALUE
	(1)	Deletions - (2)	Additions + (3)	= (4)
Current Liabilities:				
Accounts Payable	$ 23.79			$ 23.79
Current Portion of Long-Term Debt	4.16			4.16
Income Taxes Payable	1.37			1.37
Total Current Liabilities	29.32			29.32
Long-Term Debt:				
Term Loan	20.85			20.85
Revolver	18.00			18.00
Subordinated Debt & Bridge Loan	15.99			15.99
Total Long-Term Debt	54.84			54.84
Other Liabilities:	6.73			6.73
Total Liabilities	90.89			90.89
Shareholders' Equity:				
Common Stock	9.35	(9.35)		
Capital in Excess of Par Value	9.38	(9.38)		
Retained Earnings	(8.21)	8.21		
Notes Receivable	(5.99)	5.99		
Net Worth			12.48	12.48
Total Shareholders' Equity	$ 4.53	$ (4.53)	$ 12.48	$ 12.48
Total Liabilities & Equity	$ 95.42	$ (4.53)	$ 12.48	$103.37

of operating income and operating cash flow for a number of busing companies whose values have been determined through recent mergers or acquisitions (Exhibit 7-8).

First, we identified comparable acquisitions in the busing industry. For each transaction, the comparable company's earnings before interest and taxes (EBIT, or operating income), earnings before interest and taxes *plus* depreciation and amortization (EBITDA, or operating cash flow) and Business Enterprise Value were obtained. Business Enterprise Value was supplied by Securities Data Corporation. The median multiples should give us a reasonable benchmark for the multiple for Great Lakes Bus Lines. Here, the median EBIT multiple is 13.87 and the median EBITDA multiple is 6.21. By multiplying these multiples by Great Lakes' EBIT and EBITDA respectively, we can estimate Great Lakes' Business Enterprise Value, as shown in Exhibit 7-9.

Finally, since Business Enterprise Value, a measure of debt plus equity, represents the firm's *assets*, we must subtract Great Lakes' debt in order to determine its solvency, as calculated in Exhibit 7-10.

The value of Great Lakes' equity represents the amount by which the company was solvent. As presented in Exhibit 7-10, using both measures indicates that the firm was solvent by a wide margin.

Another approach to using the EBIT and EBITDA multiples is in conjunction with the total market capitalization of publicly traded firms in the same industry. Total market capitalization is defined as the share price times the number of shares plus debt. For example, at the time of Great Lakes' disputed solvency, Dakota Bus' stock was $26.50 per share, with 6,526,000 shares outstanding. Multiplying these numbers gives us a total equity value of

Exhibit 7-8. Operating Income And Cash Flows of
Busing Firms Comparable to Great Lakes
($ millions)

Company	Business Enterprise Value	EBIT	EBIT Multiple	EBITDA	EBITDA Multiple
Aztec Group	$348.37	$21.70	16.05	$39.90	8.73
Bordon Bus Lines	71.10	7.36	9.66	9.52	7.47
Commonwealth Lns	39.04	5.00	7.81	8.10	4.82
Corcoran Lines	89.20	10.87	8.21	17.39	5.13
Cross Country Bus	642.75	97.10	6.62	152.80	4.21
Inter City Lines	38.99	2.75	14.18	9.03	4.32
Lone Star Bus Co.	159.06	9.30	17.10	18.70	8.51
McTavish Bus Lines	101.30	2.89	35.05	23.56	4.30
Minnesota Group	461.60	31.30	14.75	74.30	6.21
Mountain Transp.	1,161.12	82.00	14.16	103.03	11.27
Sahara Transp.	686.78	46.40	14.80	132.80	5.17
Saturn Bus Lines	38.72	8.80	4.40	15.90	2.44
Southern Transport	25.45	1.87	13.58	2.87	8.87
Southern Bus Co.	40.03	(0.60)	NMF	2.40	16.68
Traveler Bus Lines	163.59	13.00	12.58	20.80	7.86
Median			**13.87**		**6.21**

Exhibit 7-9. Estimating Great Lakes' Business
Enterprise Value ($ millions)

	Great Lakes' Figure	x	Comparables' Median Multiple	=	Great Lakes' Business Enterprise Value
EBIT	$7.33		13.87		$101.66
EBITDA	$13.68		6.21		$84.96

Exhibit 7-10. Estimating Great Lakes' Solvency
($ millions)

		EBIT Approach	EBITDA Approach
	Business Enterprise Value	$101.66	84.96
-	Debt	58.99	58.99
=	Value of Equity	$42.67	$25.97

$172.9 million. Adding Dakota's $85.4 million in debt results in a total market "cap" of $258.3 million. In Exhibit 7-11, we have identified five publicly traded competitors of Great Lakes Bus Lines, including Dakota Bus, determined their total market capitalizations as described above, and then calculated their respective EBIT and EBITDA multiples. Using the medians of these multiples, we can obtain the equity required for measuring Great Lakes' solvency.

Just as we did earlier, we can employ these multiples for estimating the value of Great Lakes' equity by multiplying the median multiples by the respective EBIT and EBITDA values of Great Lakes, less its debt.

Exhibit 7-11. Multiples Based On Total Market
Capitalization of Great Lakes'
Competitors ($ millions)

Company	Total Market Cap	EBIT	EBIT Multiple	EBITDA	EBITDA Multiple
Dakota Bus	258.33	18.90	13.67	47.43	5.45
Fordham Lines	1,332.01	101.22	13.16	197.82	6.73
Gorsuch Bus Co.	259.71	11.58	22.43	37.99	6.84
Linder Trans.	1,221.68	58.12	21.02	173.27	7.05
Omaha Lines	1,025.43	78.09	13.13	177.07	5.79
Median Multiple			13.67		6.73

As indicated by Exhibit 7-12, the amounts by which Great Lakes Bus Lines was solvent based on the EBIT and EBITDA multiples are respectively $41.21 million and $33.08 million. They roughly match our earlier value estimates, confirming that the company was, indeed, solvent when the LBO transaction took place.

Exhibit 7-12. Estimating Great Lakes' Solvency
($ millions)

		EBIT as a Parameter	EBITDA as a Parameter
x	Great Lakes' Parameter Median Competitors' Multiple	7.33 13.67	13.68 6.73
= −	Great Lakes' B.E.V. Great Lakes' Debt	100.20 58.99	92.07 58.99
=	Great Lakes' Equity	$41.21	$33.08

3. *The discounted cash flow (DCF) approach.* Our third and final method for determining solvency is discounted cash flow analysis. It explicitly estimates the value of the firm in terms of its unique future characteristics. While the fair value balance sheet approach implicitly looks beyond the here and now, and the multiples reflect expectations, the DCF approach explicitly projects cash flows from operating activities (EBITDA), including expected changes in working capital. It also factors into "net" cash flows all anticipated capital expenditures and proceeds from divestments of firm assets.

Without getting into the minutia, we project that the net cash flow from operating and investing activities for

Great Lakes Bus Lines will look as follows for the first year under study and the years to follow:

	Year 0	Year 1	Year 2	Year 3	Year 4	Year 5	Years > 5
Cash Flow	1.703	5.085	5.056	5.262	6.7400	6.200 107.46◄	4% growth per year
Present Value	1.703	4.623	4.179	3.953	4.604	3.850 66.724	

The sum of the net present value of these cash flows (at 10%) is $89.636 million, which, after subtracting the debt, implies an equity value of $30.64 million. This confirms what our other methods have determined – that Great Lakes was solvent at the time of its leveraged buy-out.

Assessing undercapitalization. Although the firm may have been solvent at the time of the LBO transaction, the Court may still find that a fraudulent conveyance has occurred if the transaction left the firm undercapitalized. However, determining whether a firm was adequately capitalized is potentially more complex than determining whether it was solvent. While the firm's debt-to-equity ratio is relevant, there are no rigid rules, formulas or guidelines to evaluate capital adequacy. Under applicable fraudulent transfer law, "undercapitalized" means that a prudent financial expert would determine that the company lacks sufficient resources to meet its financial obligations under a reasonable range of likely outcomes.

Several tests may be used to determine whether the firm is adequately capitalized, including:

1. At the time of the LBO transaction, did the firm have sufficient cash flow to meet existing expenses plus anticipated debt service?
2. Did the firm have the financial capacity to withstand a mild recession (a likely occurrence during the life of a typical LBO loan)?
3. Did the firm have access to additional credit, or was it "tapped out?"
4. Did the firm find it necessary to delay payments to creditors immediately after the LBO transaction?

Some of these tests depend on the nature of the firm and its industry. For example, a cyclical business that is severely affected by recessions is likely to require more equity than one with relatively stable and predictable cash flows. Likewise, a firm dependent on capital investment may need substantially greater cash flow or equity than others to assure continued capital spending. Thus, the Court must evaluate a whole set of operating and financial characteristics to determine whether the firm being analyzed should be viewed as undercapitalized.

Minimizing the risk of fraudulent conveyance. The potential consequences for parties involved in a transaction, including lenders, shareholders, and providers of analysis and advice are so severe, that extreme care must be taken in structuring leveraged buyouts and other recapitalizations. This being the case, it is often useful to evaluate the firm from various perspectives, including satisfying the criteria that:

1. The firm's operating history is stable and not subject to major cyclical downturns.
2. The post-LBO debt-equity ratio is comparable to that of any other LBOs in the industry.

3. The firm will be able to pay its creditors under a reasonable set of adverse conditions.
4. The firm's cash flows support the creditworthiness of the loan; good collateral should not be a substitute for insufficient cash flows.
5. The post-LBO firm will have borrowing capacity available to it in the event of insufficient operating cash flows.
6. The firm's accrued liabilities are not so large as to impair payment to creditors and do not have to be paid too soon after the LBO transaction.
7. The post-LBO firm will be left with sufficient funds to provide for maintenance and necessary capital improvements.
8. The projections provided by the acquiring group have been carefully reviewed and verified.
9. The market conditions upon which the projections are based (e.g., price stabilization and demand) have been fully described.
10. The firm's past profits were generated as a result of operating flows, which are likely to continue, as opposed to accounting changes, which are unlikely to have a long-term effect.
11. The firm is not in a deeply troubled, turnaround situation.
12. The source of the projections used was someone in the firm able to provide a realistic portrayal of the firm's operations and financial practices, as opposed to someone without an appropriate background.
13. Assumptions, procedures and data have been reviewed by an independent third party, if at all practical.

Obviously, the relevant criteria vary from case to case. Generally, an analysis that meets these criteria provides the best possible evidence to controvert any assertion that a particular LBO constituted a fraudulent conveyance. Based on the industry and situation, however, several of the criteria may not be met and the firm would still be considered solvent and adequately capitalized.

Index

Accounting concepts, 2–5
Accounts receivable, 10
Accounts payable, definition, 14
Accrual method of accounting, 2
    matching costs and
        revenues, 5
Accrued liabilities, 14
Activity ratios, 38–41
Adjusted book value method,
    180–181
Alpha, of portfolio, 122–124;
    See also Jensen measure
Amortization of intangible as-
    sets, 17
Annuity, definition, 72; *See also*
    Future value of an annuity;
    and Present value of an
    annuity
Assets
    brand names, 18
    categories on balance sheet,
        8–13
    current vs. non-current, 9,
        11
    intangible assets, 17
Average collection period, 40–
    41; *See also* Activity ratios
Bad debts, 10
Balance sheet, 6–18
    accounting vs. economic
        values, 16
    basic equation, 16
    marking to market, 17
Bankruptcy
    bankruptcy code, 247; *See
        also* Chapter 7; and
        Chapter 11
    creditor committee, 242
    informal liquidation, 246–
        247

informal reorganization,
    242; *See also* Extension;
    Composition; and
    Creditor control
voluntary settlements
    (workouts), 242
Benchmarking investment
    performance, 126–127
Beta coefficient, 105–108
    of portfolio, 123
    See also Measuring Risk
Book value method, 176–180
Brand name value, 18
Business damages, 222–234
Business enterprise value, 188,
    199, 203
Call risk, 130
Capital asset pricing model
    (CAPM)
    applied to business
        damages, 231
    in calculating cost of equity,
        161–162
    in calculating expected
        return, 119–121
    general description, 114–15
    See also Risk
Cash, definition, 9
Cash flow
    how calculated, 204–207
    debt-free, 203, 206-208
    definition, 203
    sources of, 28–30
Cash flow statement, 26
Cash method of accounting, 2
Chapter 7 of U.S. Bankruptcy
    Code, 247, 253
    priority of claims, 254–255
Chapter 11 of U.S. Bankruptcy
    Code
    benefits to firm, 248

costs of, 249
debtor-in-possession (DIP),
  248–249
feasibility or reorganization
  plan, 250
order of claims, 251
prepackaged, 252
Characteristic line, 106; *See
  also* Beta coefficient
Churning, 147–149
Competitive analysis, 58–61
Composition, calculating cost of,
  243–245; *See also* Bankruptcy
Conservatism concept, 4
Convertible bond, 143–145
Correlation, as related to risk;
  See Diversification; and
  Risk
Cost
  cost concept, 3–4
  fixed and variable, 223
  matched to revenue, 23
  See also LIFO and FIFO
Cost of capital
  definition, 87, 156
  as discount rate, 87
  and the privately owned
    firm, 168–171
  weighted average (WACOC)
    calculation, 157
  See also Cost of Debt; Cost
    of Equity; Cost of
    Preferred Stock
Cost of debt
  after-tax calculation 161
  definition and calculation
    157–161
Cost of equity, 161–167
Cost of goods sold, 11
Cost of preferred stock, 171–
  172
Creditor control, 246

Current ratio, 37–38; *See also*
  Liquidity ratios
Damages
  bases for, 211–212
  involving non-disclosure,
    236
  See also Wrongful death;
    Business damages;
    Securities damage; Non-
    disclosure
Debt ratio, 41–42; *See also*
  Leverage ratios
Default risk, on bonds, 129–
  130
Debt securities; *See* Securities
Debtor-in-possession, 248–249
Depreciation
  definition, 22
  double declining balance
    method, 13–14
  straight line vs. accelerated,
    12–13
Derivatives
  convertible bond, 143–145
  definition, 135–136
  forward and future
    contracts, 143
  hedging with, example, 144
  stock index options, 143
  swap, 143
  warrants, 145
  See also Options
Discounted cash flow (DCF)
  valuation, 200–206
  applied to fraudulent
    conveyance case, 207–
    210
  in determining solvency,
    270–271
Discounting, as backward
  compounding, 71
Discount rate

in business damages cases,
    231
risk-free rate, 120, 231
how selected, 86–87, 93
in wrongful death cases,
    219
as yield-to-maturity, 159
See also Internal rate of
    return (IRR)
Diversification
and imprudent
    management, 150
and reducing risk, 108–113
Dividend growth model, 162–
163. *See also* Cost of
Equity
Dual-aspect concept, 2–3
Earnings before interest and
taxes (EBIT), definition, 47
EBIT
in assessing solvency, 267–
    271
multiple valuation, 186–
    190
EBITDA
in assessing solvency, 267–
    271
multiple valuation, 190–
    193
Economic value added (EVA),
48
Entity concept, 3
Equity value, calculation, 199,
204
Exchange rate risk, 130
Extension, calculating costs of,
243–244; *See also Bank-
ruptcy*
Failure to disclose, 151
Fair salable value, in cases of
fraudulent conveyance, 262
Form 8-K, 30
Form 10-K, 30

Form, 10-Q, 30
Forward and future contracts,
143
FIFO
and book value valuations,
    179
matching costs to revenues,
    24
Financial calculator, and time
value solutions, 87–94
Financial distress, 239–241.
See also Bankruptcy
Financial leverage
effect on cost of equity, 164
impact on the bottom line,
    165
management discussion, 31
requirements for public
    companies, 30
See also Balance sheet; In-
    come statement; Cash
    flow statement
Fixed asset turnover ratio, 39–
40; *See also* Activity ratios
Fixed charge coverage ratio,
43–44; *See also* Leverage
ratios
Fraud on the market, 151–154
Fraudulent conveyance, 257–
274
assessing solvency, 259–
    263
assessing undercapitaliza-
    tion, 271–72
fair consideration, 259
fair salable value, 262
methods for determining
    solvency, 263–271
minimizing risk, 272–274
Future value of a present single
sum, 65–70
Future value of an annuity due,
72-76

Future value of an ordinary
    annuity, 76–79
Generally Accepted Accounting
    Principles (GAAP), 6
    flexibility in determining
        earnings, 25
Going-concern concept, 3
Goodwill
    balance sheet treatment,
        17
    difficulty of valuation 12
    how arises, 11
Gordon dividend model, 197
Gross margin ratio, 45; *See
    also* Profitability ratios
Historical cost, 16–17
    and distortions in book
        value valuations, 177–
        180
    and income, 23
    as source of difference
        between accounting vs.
        economic value, 16
Hurdle rate; *See* Cost of capital
Imprudent management, in
    securities litigation, 150–
    151
Income statement, 18–26
Industry ratios, 50–51
Intangible assets, 17–18
Interest rate risk, 131
Internal rate of return (IRR),
    96-99
Inventory, definition, 10
Inventory turnover ratio, 40;
    See also Activity ratios
Item 303 of Regulation S-K, 32,
    34
Jensen measure, 122–124
Leverage, financial, concept of,
    47
Leverage ratios, 41–45
Liabilities

accrued, 22
current vs. long-term, 13
key categories, 13–14
off balance sheet, 261
LIFO
    and book value valuations,
        179
    matching costs to revenues,
        24
Liquidity
    of assets, 7
    ratios, 36–38; *See also*
        Ratio analysis
    requirements in financial
        statements, 32
    risk for bondholders, 130
Marketable securities,
    definition, 10
Market multiple approach, 264
Matching concept
    in accounting, 5
    recognition of expenses, 21
Materiality concept, 4–5
Money-measurement concept, 3
Net income
    how determined, 19
    economic vs. accounting
        earnings, 23–26
Net present value (NPV)
    in business valuation, 202–
        203
    calculation, 94–96
Nominal growth rate, 215
Non-current assets, accounting
    for, 11
Non-disclosure damages, 236–
    237
Notes payable, 14
Number of days payable ratio,
    44–45; *See also* Leverage
    ratios
Options
    contract features, 137

as derivatives, 136
valuation and break even
    calculations, 137–143
Owners' equity, 14–16
Paid-in capital, definition, 15
P/E multiple valuation, 183–
    185
Portfolio
    alpha, 122–124
    beta, 123
    turnover ratio, 148–149;
        See also Churning
Prepaid expenses, definition,
    11
Present value
    of a future single sum, 70-
        72
    of an annuity due, 84–87
    of an ordinary annuity, 79–
        84
    of lost earnings, 219–222
Procter & Gamble
    case against Bankers
        Trust, 145–147
    derivative strategy, 135
Profitability ratios, 45–48
Profit & loss (P&L) statement.
    See Income statement
Profit margin ratio, 46; *See also*
    Profitability ratios
Prospectus, on new securities,
    30–31
Purchasing power risk, 130
Quality of management, 61.
Quick ratio, 38; *See also*
    Liquidity ratios
Ratio analysis, 36–58
Realization concept, 5
Real growth rate, 215
Red herring. *See* Prospectus on
    new securities
Replacement value, as market
    value proxy, 180

Retained earnings, 15–16
Return
    arithmetic average,
        calculation, 116
    capital asset pricing model
        used to calculate, 119–
        121
    expected rate of, definition,
        117
    geometric average,
        calculation, 116–117
    rate of, calculation, 115–
        118
    risk-adjusted, 122
    risk-free rate, 120
    yield-to-maturity, 132–133
    See also Jensen measure;
        Treynor measure;
        Sharpe measure; and
        Benchmarking
        performance
Return on equity, 47–48; *See
    also* Profitability ratios
Return on total assets, 46–47;
    See also Profitability ratios
Revenues, when recognized, 21
Risk
    beta coefficient, 105–108
    capital asset pricing model,
        114–115
    debt securities, 129–132
    investors' definition, 102–
        103
    measurement, 104–108
    reduction through
        diversification, 108–113
    risk-adjusted return, 122
    risk/return relationship,
        113–115
    systematic and
        unsystematic, 103
    total risk, calculation, 104
Securities

causes for litigation, 101;
147–154. *See also*
Churning; Imprudent
management;
Suitability; Failure to
disclose; and Fraud on
the market
damages cases, 235
debt securities
indices, 128
market values and
interest rates, 132
risks for bondholders
129–132
types and features,
127–129
valuation, 133–135
yield-to-maturity, 132–
133
Securities and Exchange
Commission (SEC)
enforcement, 33
financial statement
requirements for public
companies, 30
Security market line, 114–115
Sharpe measure, 125–126
Standard deviation, definition,
104–105; *See also*
Measuring Risk
Solvency
assessing in cases of
fraudulent conveyance,
259–263
methods for determining,
263–271
Stockholders' equity; *See* Owners' equity
Stock index options, 143
Swap, 143
Systematic and unsystematic
risk; *See* Risk
Terminal value, 202

Times interest earned ratio, 43;
See also Leverage ratios
Time value of money
and financial calculator,
87–94
See Future value; Present
value; Future value of
an annuity; Present
value of an annuity; Net
present value; and
Internal rate of return
Total asset turnover ratio, 39;
See also Activity ratios
Trend analysis, example using
ratios, 51–54
Treynor measure, 124–125
Undercapitalization, in case of
fraudulence conveyance,
271–272
Valuation
adjusted book value
method, 180–181
book value method, 176–
180
capitalization of dividends
and cash flows, 196–
199
issues for attorneys, 176
use of multiples, 181–195;
See P/E multiple; EBIT
multiple; and EBITDA
multiple
Weighted average cost of
capital (WACOC)
and business valuation,
197–198
calculation, 167–168
Working capital
cash squeezes, 29
definition, 37
Warrant, as derivative, 145
Wrongful death, 213–214
calculation of damages, 214

determining discount rate,
219
Yield-to-maturity
on debt securities, 132–133
as proxy for cost of debt,
159